Contents

Foreword

PUBLISHING A COLLECTION of essays devoted to Conrad's short fiction does not speak for itself. More than any other writer, Conrad is perceived as a novelist whose forays into short fiction are at best preliminary, crude exercises in preparation for the great novels and at worst, hackwork done for material survival, unworthy of his greater literary accomplishments. This view owes much to the close association of short-story writing with commercial and popular magazines during the twentieth century's first two decades, which generated a general view of the genre as material made to order, commodified, commercialized, intended mainly to entertain and distract the masses, and levelled into a show of verbal craftsmanship. Conrad's own disparaging view of his short fiction did much to propagate this general conception: he refers to these works as "silly short stories" (*CL*3: 297); he claims that they are "not studies – they touch no problem. They are just stories in which I've tried to be simply entertaining" (*CL*4: 29-30); and he dismisses various individual stories with a reference to "secondhand Conradese" (*CL*1: 301).

Can we take Conrad at his word and follow his dismissal of these stories with a nod towards the marketplace, his creditors, the pressures of a growing family, ill-health, and other all-too-understandable if not entirely admirable facts of life? The present collection of essays offers an alternative, more complex view. Conrad's disparaging references to his short fiction evidence remarkably little anxiety (a notable change from his epistolary agonizing over his novels) and indicate no sense of artistic discomfort or embarrassment that would have been natural for a highly self-conscious, relentlessly critical mind. It may well be that his conscious intention to address his short fiction to the popular market had a liberating effect on his writing process and that the relative relaxation of critical self-reflection may have paradoxically enabled the radical narrative experimentation that characterizes a number of the short stories.

While many of Conrad's short stories were indeed written with an eye on the marketplace, he was, to put it simply, constitutionally unable to produce pulp fiction. Much as he tried to produce formulaic pieces that would satisfy the popular taste for exotic settings, romance, and melodrama, the end-product would always turn out to be a little less satisfactorily marketable and somewhat more æsthetically intriguing than it was meant to be. Although written for popular consumption, the stories are rarely trivial or formulaic: they are often generically ambivalent, subverting the very conventions that would have slotted them comfortably into popular generic categories.

In addition to the obvious seductions of the marketplace, it is not hard to see why Conrad found this form congenial. Short story theories are notoriously helpless when it comes to generic definitions, and the most enduring attempt at defining the genre is still the most startlingly simple – a definition based on the time it takes to read the story or (as summarily put by one of these critics) "a definition by the seat of one's pants." These difficulties notwithstanding, it is generally agreed that the kind of short fiction that emerged during the last decade of the nineteenth century and became widely popular during the first three decades of the twentieth anticipates and encapsulates many of the Modernist novel's "Impressionist" characteristics: the limitation and foregrounding of point-of-view; an emphasis on inner experience; a reliance on metaphor and metonymy; an elliptical treatment of traditional plot elements and chronological ordering. Often labelled an "Impressionist," Conrad is strategically placed for a study of the relationship between these two Modernist genres, and much of his short fiction anticipates the more radical and experimental writing of his novels.

Perhaps the most pertinent point of conjunction is the "isolating" tendency of the short story. As Frank O'Connor, a master of the genre, writes: "the novel can still adhere to the classical concept of a civilized society, of man as an animal who lives in a community … but the short story remains by its very nature remote from the community – romantic, individualistic, and intransigent" (*The Lonely Voice*, 1962: 21). The viewpoint of the Modernist short story is that of the outsider; its position is on the margins of society; its material is a fragment of what was once a communal web. Conrad's short fiction, like his novels, revolves on this nostalgia for the sense of community and the awareness of its loss.

A second point of conjunction is the genre's distinctive orality: unlike the novel that, according to Mary Louise Pratt, often foregrounds its own "writtenness," short fiction is closely related to the living voice, to spoken language, to oral narrative. This orality, perceived as generically related to the short story is, in fact, one of the most distinctive traits of Conrad's work, both in his short fiction and novels, which often revolve on narrative situations and foreground problems of narrative authority, interpretation, and voice.

Most of the essays in this special issue of *The Conradian* not only make a case for re-evaluating some of Conrad's short stories but also take new and broader directions, reflecting a novel focus on the intersection of culture and literary production: the relationship between the advertising industry and the production of literary texts; an emergent awareness of the cinema as a new æsthetic challenge; the vexed question of Conrad's alleged misogyny and his problematic treatment of love; the profound ambivalence of Conrad's politics; and his uneasy position in relation to the ethos of empire. It is, perhaps, the conception of culture in a broad sense, including ideology, institutions, and discursive practices, that allows for reinterpreting some of the interesting oddities of these ostensibly commodified texts.

At the conclusion of this project, the question that hovered over the conception of this issue – whether the short fiction written by the great novelist can indeed be read as mere "secondhand Conradese" – has become vastly more complex and intriguing for the editorial team that has had the pleasure of compiling this volume. As ever, the last word is left with our readers.

Daphna Erdinast-Vulcan

Contributors

JÜRGEN KRAMER is Professor of British Cultural Studies at the Universität Dortmund. His main research areas include the sea as a cultural space, transatlantic slavery, the literature of the Pacific, cultural memory, and anti-colonial resistance. Among his publications are *Cultural and Intercultural Studies* (1990) and *British Cultural Studies* (1997), and since 1994 he has co-edited the *Journal for the Study of British Cultures.* His most recent Conrad work is "Conrad's Crews Revisited," in *Fictions of the Sea: Critical Perspectives on the Ocean in British Literature and Culture*, edited by Bernhard Klein (Aldershot: Ashgate, 2002).

CEDRIC WATTS is Research Professor of English at the University of Sussex. His many books on Conrad include *The Deceptive Text* (1984), *Joseph Conrad: A Literary Life* (1989), *Joseph Conrad: "Nostromo"* (1990), *A Preface to Conrad* (2nd edition, 1993), and *Joseph Conrad* (1994). He has written widely on other writers, including Shakespeare.

SEMA POSTACIOGLU-BANON teaches English at the Università Ca' Foscari in Venice. She has published translations of and articles on Conrad, V. S. Naipaul, and Melville. Her doctoral thesis focused on *The Secret Agent* and *Under Western Eyes.* In Venice she has organized literary film festivals (on Conrad, Kipling, and Wells) and is currently working on a book to be called *Visions of Progress.*

PAUL MARCH-RUSSELL teaches in the School of English at Kent University, Canterbury. He has published on Modernism and on the Gothic, and is currently writing a book on the Modernist short story, including references to Conrad.

MICHAEL LUCAS teaches English Language and Literature at the Universidad del Bío-Bío in Chillán, Chile. His initial interest in Conrad was linguistic, focusing on Conrad as a very advanced non-native user of English specifically intending to write fiction. His essays on Conrad have appeared in journals and volumes of conference papers, and he has published *Aspects of Conrad's Literary Language* in the series Conrad: Eastern and Western Perspectives.

STEPHEN DONOVAN, a postdoctoral researcher at the Blekinge Institute of Technology in Karlskrona, Sweden, is currently living in New York City. His work has appeared in *Journal of Modern Literature* and *The Conradian*, and is forthcoming in *James Joyce Quarterly*. He was awarded the Juliet McLauchlan Essay Prize by the Joseph Conrad Society (UK) in 1999. Palgrave will publish his *Joseph Conrad and Popular Culture* in 2004.

MARK D. LARABEE, a commander in the United States Navy, has taught at the United States Naval Academy in Annapolis, Maryland, as a Senior Instructor of English. His essays on Conrad have appeared in *Studies in the Novel*, *CEA Critic*, and in the recent *Approaches to Teaching Conrad's "Heart of Darkness" and "The Secret Sharer"* (MLA).

JEREMY HAWTHORN is Professor of Modern British Literature at the Norwegian University of Science and Technology, Trondheim. The author of *Joseph Conrad: Language and Fictional Self-Consciousness* (1979) and *Joseph Conrad: Narrative Technique and Ideological Commitment* (1990), he has edited *Under Western Eyes* and *The Shadow-Line* in the new Oxford World's Classics series (both 2003).

JENNIFER TURNER completed her undergraduate degree at Clare College, Cambridge, before moving to the University of Hull for an M.A. in "Women and Literature in English." She is now in the final year of her Ph.D. programme, writing on "The Female Spectre: A Freudian Analysis of Women in the Life and Works of Joseph Conrad."

What the Country Doctor "did not see": The Limits of the Imagination in "Amy Foster"

Jürgen Kramer
Universität Dortmund

> Nor bring, to see me cease to live,
> Some doctor full of phrase and fame,
> To shake his sapient head and give
> The ill he cannot cure a name.
>
> Matthew Arnold, "The Wish"

> He that has eyes to see and ears to hear may convince himself that no mortal can keep a secret. If his lips are silent, he chatters with his finger-tips; betrayal oozes out of him at every pore.
>
> Sigmund Freud, "Fragment of an Analysis of a Case of Hysteria"

OVER THE PAST fifteen years Conrad's "Amy Foster" (1901) has achieved some prominence among critics for a variety of reasons. Its different versions (Fraser 1988), its impressionist aspects (Epstein 1991), its dialogic and intercultural dimensions (Krajka 1990; Carabine 1992), its nature as "a colonialist story in reverse" (Ruppel 1996: 126), and its exploration of the trauma of "culture shock" (Finkelstein 2000; Shaffer 2000) have all garnered critical attention. In spite of their different foci these readings share the assumption that either Yanko or Amy or both are at the story's centre. Myrtle Hooper (1996), while not denying the protagonists' centrality, focuses on the way in which Kennedy, the principal I-narrator, shapes his narrative and thereby invites the collusion of his listener-visitor, the nameless frame-narrator, and male readers and critics. This interesting thesis is worth contesting as well as expanding on.

The story's plot need not be rehearsed here. After their prolonged courtship Yanko and Amy marry and, eventually, have a boy. It is from this point – after a period of "two or three years" (*Typhoon*, 117) – that things apparently go "wrong." The following passage from Kennedy's discourse summarizes a conversation with Yanko:

> He told me that "women were funny." I had heard already of domestic differences. People were saying that Amy Foster was beginning to find out what sort of man she had married. He looked upon the sea with indifferent, unseeing eyes. His wife had snatched the child out of his arms one day as he sat on the doorstep crooning to it a song such as the mothers sing to babies in his mountains. She seemed to think he was doing it some harm. Women are funny. And she had objected to him praying aloud in the evening. Why? He expected the boy to repeat the prayer aloud after him by-and-by, as he used to do after his old father when he was a child – in his own country. And I discovered he longed for their boy to grow up so that he could have a man to talk with in that language that to our ears sounded so disturbing, so passionate, and so bizarre. Why his wife should dislike the idea he couldn't tell. But that would pass, he said. And tilting his head knowingly, he tapped his breastbone to indicate that she had a good heart: not hard, not fierce, open to compassion, charitable to the poor! (137)

Kennedy, whose intelligence, according to the frame-narrator, is of "a scientific order" (106), provides an accentuated description of the classical "critical incidents" of a particular family dynamic: the process of early triangulation (which prepares and ideally merges into the Oedipus complex). An approximate summary could be that human beings are born into a cultural order to which they must be painfully introduced. In this process they have to learn two interrelated things: first, that their early immediate access to "reality" (which they imagine to have had in the symbiotic relationship with the "mother") is transformed into one mediated by language; and, secondly, that becoming part of culture implies being recognized and accepting oneself as either male or female.

These processes can be painful not only for the child but also for the parents. With the birth of the baby, the male partner must transform his role of lover/husband into "husband-and-father," that is, he has to accept that, at least for some time, he is not or, at least, not the only one at the centre of his partner's affection. It is important that, when the infant eventually becomes aware of this "third person," the pains of the "narcissistic wound" have been integrated by the father so that they are not vented on the baby. The mother, in turn, originally "experienced" by the infant as an extension of his or her body, has to separate herself from the baby to a certain extent (by, for example, stopping breastfeeding) in order to allow insertion into the socio-cultural realm represented by a third person – any third person, but usually the father. The presence of this individual who makes himself felt as a third person and communicates with the baby eventually transforms the mother-child-dyad into a triad or a triangle – hence the term used above.

The difficulties of these developmental processes should not be underestimated: they involve three persons, who in their interactions have to negotiate their previous experiences, particularly in the case of the parents, and their familial proximity. Clearly, further differences of, for example, class or ethnicity, which over-determine the sexual difference between mother and father, deepen the profound complexity of these processes.

In the particular "case" of Yanko, according to what we learn from Kennedy, Yanko does what is "normal," striving to introduce his son to his culture by talking and singing to him as well as praying for him. Amy, however, reacts as if her son were being alienated from her. This, in fact, is the case, and in any normal construction this is inevitable. She feels doubly threatened, however, because, on the one hand, her role as mother is transformed by Yanko's "entrance" into her relationship with Johnny, and, on the other, and more importantl*y*, the fact that she does not know Yanko's language implies that she may be excluded from a significant part of the triangle and, thereby, have reduced significance in her child's future development. Amy reacts by unwittingly replacing Yanko by the baby in her affections: Johnny requires the same amount of care, compassion, and love as Yanko did when he was "born again" from the shipwreck and washed ashore. But while Yanko has "grown up," learned "to speak intelligibly" (123) and, in due course, made demands in accordance with his social role and function within this nuclear family, Johnny himself, although Kennedy notices "his fluttered air of a bird in a snare" (142), has yet to disrupt the maternal bond.

Yanko, as the reader learns, insists on being accepted as husband *and* father until he falls ill. Kennedy diagnoses "lung trouble" and adds: "He was tough, but I daresay he was not acclimatized as well as I had supposed. It was a bad winter; and, of course, these mountaineers do get fits of homesickness; and a state of depression would make him vulnerable" (138). To diagnose "lack of acclimatization" after three years of however initially precarious residence in England more than begs the question, but as Kennedy is apparently prepared to take into account some psychic origins of Yanko's illness, it is worth pursuing this further. Homesickness and depression can engender vulnerability to infections. But should we not pay more attention to where in the body they occur, and what, in context, then, does "lung trouble" signify? Breathing, a rhythmic action, is set in motion when the umbilical cord is cut, and breathing in and out is at the basis of our most fundamental exchange process: the body is supplied with oxygen while carbon dioxide is emitted. Moreover, the rhythm of breathing in and out is related to other alternating processes such as tension ("in") and relaxation ("out"). Although we can hold our breath for a certain length of time, we cannot altogether stop it of our own free will. In the nature of constant give-and-take lies our breath's significance. We cannot help but communicate with the world we live in. And the degree to which we do this becomes clearer, if we realize that the body possesses two "contact organs": the skin and the inner surface of the lungs. While the former is only one to two square metres in size, the latter is around seventy square metres. Yanko's "lung trouble" can be read as a result of the fact that the "healthy" mixture of tension and relaxation in his self, of give-and-take in interpersonal communication, of exchange with his family and community is seriously disturbed, and his rising fever signals his attempt to protect himself against whatever it is (lack of or the cessation of mutual understanding) that makes him "gasp for breath" or "takes his breath away." If, in his fever, he speaks in his mother tongue instead of English, this suggests that, in his conflict with Amy, he insists both on the communicative value of his language and culture *and* on the significance of his role in the family triangle. And, when Kennedy finds him on the morning after Amy has left him, it makes sense that the fever has also left Yanko, "taking with it the heat of life" (141). Yanko has realized that by fleeing him she has finally disrupted the rudimentary forms of communication that they may still have had. He knows that his act of resistance can no longer touch her, and he dies a truly "broken" man: he is without the family he came from and the one he started, and he resignedly resorts to English to explain his fate to the narrator and to ask, incorrectly but movingly, for God's mercy.

And what of Amy? Myrtle Hooper suggests that Kennedy "never attempts to represent Amy's point of view" (1996: 56) but also attributes a certain "inertness" of mind to her (*Typhoon*, 107) and, in effect, silences her "so that she won't interfere" (1996: 64) with his version of Yanko's tragedy. Arguing against Kennedy's statement that, confronted with "the terror, the unreasonable terror, of that man she could not understand" there was nothing in Amy "but the maternal instinct and that unaccountable fear" (139), Hooper correctly contends that Amy's fear could be accounted for because, in her eyes, Yanko was turning the child into a stranger, thus replicating his own alienness and difference (see 1996: 60-61). This implies that Amy, in contrast to what Kennedy suggests and the frame-narrator apparently corroborates (see 107), is anything but dull. She understands very well if, perhaps, not literally that Yanko is making demands not only for himself in his illness but also with regard to his role and function in the family. When she attempts to ignore these, he confronts her. Yanko's thirst is complementary to his hunger for bread when he is washed ashore; that both demands are articulated in his mother tongue signals their connection. But while Yanko's use of his mother tongue in their first encounter is an expression of his inability to make himself understood, his latter (feverish) use of it signifies both his grown sense of his otherness and his conviction that he must admit to and abide by it. Within the context of their small patriarchally constructed family Amy can do only two things: she can either submit to Yanko's wishes or flee. She opts for the latter because in this way she can exchange one love object (her husband) for another one (her son), while when she allows Yanko to introduce Johnny to his culture, she discerns that she may eventually lose both love objects. Moreover, if we accept Kennedy's view that Amy's love of Yanko "was love as the Ancients understood it: an irresistible and fateful impulse – a possession!" (110), her reaction to Yanko's behaviour can additionally be read as fuelled by intense jealousy. According to Hooper:

> Kennedy's loyalties, as doctor and as friend, motivate him to attempt to define and locate his relationship with Yanko, to

> pay tribute to it. ... If Kennedy's narrative brings Yanko (back) into being, it does so in order to compensate for his failure at the time to protect and secure the precarious social existence Yanko achieved in the village community. (1996: 62)

True though this is, there is more to Kennedy's tale than a sense of the community's and his own failure. The discussion that follows questions readings of the story that claim to find "imaginative insight" in Kennedy and, perhaps, only in him (see MacLauchlan 1978: 4) or that see Kennedy as "'blind" ... though sympathetic to Yanko" (Shaffer 2000: 172). As Andreach observes, "the story is really about the doctor's response to the events" (1965: 268).

In order to understand that the narrative is more than about individual and communal failures to understand or to feel, we need to relate two passages to each other. The first from the beginning describes when Kennedy and his visitor meet Amy for the first time:

> Kennedy pulled up to a walk. A woman, in full sunlight, was throwing a dripping blanket over a line stretched between two old apple-trees. ... the doctor raised his voice over the hedge: "How's your child, Amy?"
>
> I had the time to see her dull face, red, not with a mantling blush, but as if her flat cheeks had been vigorously slapped, and to take in the squat figure, the scanty, dusty brown hair drawn into a tight knot at the back of the head. She looked quite young. With a distinct catch in her breath, her voice sounded low and timid.
>
> "He's well, thank you."
>
> We trotted again. "A young patient of yours," I said; and the doctor, flicking the chestnut absently, muttered, "Her husband used to be."
>
> "She seems a dull creature," I remarked, listlessly.
>
> "Precisely," said Kennedy. "She is very passive. It's enough to look at the red hands hanging at the end of those short arms, at those slow, prominent brown eyes, to know the inertness of her mind – an inertness that one would think made it everlastingly safe from all the surprises of imagination. And yet which of us is safe? At any rate, such as you see her, she had enough imagination to fall in love." (107)

The passage establishes an agreement between the two narrators *and* suggests a picture of Amy to the reader: she is dull, passive, inert, and "everlastingly safe from the surprises of the imagination." The one exception is the proverbial exception to the rule. The way in which these two men talk about Amy is misogynous in depriving her of her human dignity and reducing her to being a "dull creature." To begin with, Kennedy does not ask her how she herself is, but how her son is. Little wonder, then, that her face is red "as if her flat cheeks had been vigorously slapped." Hooper interprets this as a sign of a "punishment Amy has endured" (1996: 56), but it could be more convincingly read as a sign of anger (which also causes the "catch in her breath"). Amy feels slighted and despised. More importantly, she realizes that Kennedy's inquiry after Johnny is aimed at recalling their memories of that fateful night on which Yanko died and of the fact that, terrifying as Yanko may have been, it was she who let him die helplessly.

The second passage is near the end when Kennedy visits Yanko in his illness:

> "I gave her certain directions; and going outside, I said again that he ought to be in bed upstairs. She wrung her hands. 'I couldn't. I couldn't. He keeps on saying something – I don't know what.' With the memory of all the talk against the man that had been dinned into her ears, I looked at her narrowly. I looked into her short-sighted eyes, at her dumb eyes that once in her life had seen an enticing shape, but seemed, staring at me, to see nothing at all now. But I saw she was uneasy.
>
> "'What's the matter with him?' she asked in a sort of vacant trepidation. 'He doesn't look very ill. I never did see anybody look like this before. . . .'
>
> "'Do you think,' I asked indignantly, 'he is shamming?'
>
> "'I can't help it, sir,' she said, stolidly. And suddenly she clapped her hands and looked right and left. 'And there's the baby. I am so frightened. He wanted me just now to give him the baby. I can't understand what he says to it.'
>
> "'Can't you ask a neighbour to come in to-night?' I asked.
>
> "'Please, sir, nobody seems to care to come,' she muttered, dully resigned all at once.
>
> "I impressed upon her the necessity of the greatest care, and then had to go. There was a good deal of sickness that

> winter. 'Oh, I hope he won't talk!' she exclaimed softly just as I was going away.
>
> "I don't know how it is I did not see – but I didn't."
>
> (138-39)

The passage reveals why Kennedy discriminates against Amy, why he "silences" her in his tale, and, most importantly, why he tells the tale at all. Responding to some of his visitor's casual questions, he attempts to tell Yanko and Amy's story as if he were a neutral observer capable of setting the record straight for once and all. And he is supported by his friend, the frame-narrator, who praises not only his wealth of experience, particularly of foreign countries, and his scientific intelligence, but also his "unappeasable curiosity" (106). But Kennedy is at least a participant-observer because he is involved in the tale he is telling. The key to his attitude is in the sentence: "I don't know how it is I did not see – but I didn't." That is to say he lacks the necessary imagination to comprehend and, perhaps, intervene in the situation in one way or another; instead he leaves Amy alone with her ill husband. His long practice as a country doctor suggests an acquaintance with comparable family conflicts, and although he is the only one to know anything about mediating between different cultures, he fails to "see" that he has to act. His question from the very beginning "which of us is safe?" (107) cuts both ways: it refers to the "surprises of the imagination" (107) which, indeed, may inspire us (as when Amy falls in love with Yanko) but which may also desert us when we most need them.

Kennedy's failure to "see" is all the more striking because of his scathing remarks about Smith who caught Yanko on his arrival and locked him in: "He was not imaginative enough to ask himself whether the man might not be perishing with cold and hunger" (121). And although (or is it because?) he can see now (as the narrator of the story) what he did not see then (when he participated in its action), he cannot look it in the face. Instead he must blame somebody else. When Kennedy mentions his certifying "heart-failure" (141) as the immediate cause of Yanko's death, he adds meaningfully that Yanko's "heart must have indeed failed him" (141) implying that someone else, his wife – typically imaged as "the heart" – failed him. Thus, Amy, who was puzzled by the dynamics of the situation in her family and asked Kennedy for advice, is blamed for Yanko's death and denied a voice of her own. Looked at more closely, however, Kennedy's diagnosis is significant in its general lack of meaning. It is the typical one given by a doctor when he cannot think of anything better or when further investigations are deemed unnecessary.[1] If there is a redeeming feature in Kennedy it is that he has been as much haunted by what happened as Amy has (see Schwarz 1968: 143). This is why he tells his story: he approaches his trauma by making it the elusive topic of a narrative embedded in a conversation. Realizing this, the frame-narrator, in turn, gives due prominence to Kennedy by introducing him to the reader in his narrative's very first sentence (*Typhoon*, 105).

One final train of thought. A male author of Polish origin (Conrad), living in England and writing in English (his third language), employs a (nameless, but certainly English) male frame-narrator who listens to another male narrator, his friend, an English country doctor (Kennedy[2]) with wide travelling experience (like the author), who tells a family story in which a young man from the Polish provinces and a young woman from the English countryside first fall in love with each other and then, after the birth of their son, cannot cope with their family conflicts, as a result of which the man dies. In a letter to H.-D. Davray, one of his French translators, Conrad wrote that the story's central idea was "différence essentielle des races" [the essential difference of the races] (*CL2*: 399). But what appears to be obvious and could arguably be connected to Conrad's life may be misleading, and perhaps the story is not so much about differences of the *races*, to invoke Conrad's nineteenth-century construction of "racial" difference, as about differences of the *sexes* and their functions within the patriarchal family unit. After all, Conrad himself had originally planned to call his story "The Husband" or "The Castaway" (*CL2*: 330), titles that would have emphasized the narrative's already dominant male perspective. In this context calling the story "Amy Foster" can be read in two ways: either Amy is regarded as central, the story's main culprit (to Kennedy, father and son appear like birds in a net [137, 142]) who is silenced and whose

[1] Finkelstein argues that this "constitutes a betrayal of the literal truth nearly equivalent to Marlow's lie to Kurtz's Intended" (2000: 27).

[2] The name is Irish and although nothing in the text gives prominence to Kennedy's Irishness, the mere hint of it may serve to underline his difference from the villagers.

silence is read as obstinacy, or the title, in calling our attention to a woman without a voice of her own in Kennedy's story, involuntarily demonstrates that the power of men resides in the patience of women. The first reading would most certainly be Conrad's, but fortunately the text also allows the second.

Kennedy, I should like to argue, neither Yanko nor Amy, is really at the heart of the story. In truly Marlovian fashion, the teller dominates the tale: Kennedy feels prompted by some chance remark to tell this particular story, he tells it in his way, and the story as told serves his self-fashioning more than that of the story's protagonists. The question that plagues him is, as we have seen, how to be inspired and not deserted by the "surprises of imagination," which is to say, how to prove oneself in the face of adversity. In this respect Kennedy resembles Marlow who cannot fathom what made Jim jump from the deck of the *Patna*, and yet knows that he himself is not "safe" either. (Brierly has the same self-doubt and because of this commits suicide.) Moreover, Kennedy's pride in his profession and in the knowledge he has derived from his travelling experiences instead of alleviating his sense of failure only heightens it. But more importantly, his failure indicates a lack: as far as we can gather, he is unmarried. Perhaps he "didn't see" what there was to be seen in Yanko's illness because he lacked a knowledge of family life. And perhaps in re-creating Yanko's story and in identifying with his plight (while blaming Amy for it), and in taking a constant interest in Yanko's son, Kennedy succeeds, if only momentarily, in creating a family of a kind for himself.

Works cited

Andreach, Robert J. "The Two Narrators of 'Amy Foster.'" *Studies in Short Fiction* 2 (1965): 262-69.

Carabine, Keith. "'Irreconcilable Differences': England as an 'Undiscovered Country' in Conrad's 'Amy Foster.'" In *The Ends of the Earth: 1876-1918*, edited by Simon Gatrell. 187-204. London – Atlantic Highlands, NJ: Ashfield Press, 1992.

Conrad, Joseph. *Typhoon and Other Stories.* Dent's Collected Edition. London: J. M. Dent and Sons, 1950.

Epstein, Hugh. "'Where He Is Not Wanted': Impression and Articulation in 'The Idiots' and 'Amy Foster.'" *Conradiana* 23.3 (1991): 217-32.

Finkelstein, Sue. "Hope and Betrayal: A Psychoanalytic Reading of 'Amy Foster.'" *Conradiana* 32.1 (2000): 20-30.

Fraser, Gail. "Conrad's Revisions to 'Amy Foster.'" *Conradiana* 20.3 (1988): 181-93.

Herndon, Richard. "The Genesis of Conrad's 'Amy Foster.'" *Studies in Philology* 58.3 (1960): 549-66.

Hooper, Myrtle. "'Oh, I Hope He Won't Talk': Narrative and Silence in 'Amy Foster.'" *The Conradian* 21.2 (1996): 51-64.

Krajka, Wiesław. "The Dialogue of Cultures in Joseph Conrad's 'Amy Foster.'" *New Comparison* 9 (1990): 149-57.

McLauchlan, Juliet. "'Amy Foster' – Echoes from Conrad's Own Experience?" *The Polish Review* 23.3 (1978): 3-8.

Pinsker, Sanford. "'Amy Foster': A Reconsideration." *Conradiana* 9 (1977): 179-86.

Ruppel, Richard. "Yanko Goorall in the Heart of Darkness: 'Amy Foster' as Colonialist Text." *Conradiana* 28.2 (1996): 126-32.

Schwarz, Daniel R. *The Function of the Narrator in Conrad's Shorter Fiction.* Ph.D. diss., Brown University, 1968.

Shaffer, Brian W. "Swept from the Sea: Trauma and Otherness in Conrad's 'Amy Foster.'" *Conradiana* 32.3 (2000): 163-76.

Fraudulent Signifiers: Saussure and the Sixpence in "Karain"

Cedric Watts
University of Sussex

THIS ESSAY HAS three parts. The first considers some notions attributed to Ferdinand de Saussure, among them the concept of the arbitrary sign. The second discusses a complex "signifier," the gilt sixpence, in Conrad's tale "Karain." The third offers a brief conclusion.

I

In literary theory during the last forty years or so, one of the most influential works has undoubtedly been *Cours de linguistique générale* attributed to Ferdinand de Saussure (1857-1913), who lectured on linguistics at the Université de Genève between 1906 and 1911. The volume was published posthumously in Paris and Lausanne in 1916; an English translation by Wade Baskin, *Course in General Linguistics*, was published in 1959. Countless critical books and essays have been influenced by its terms and ideas: we have become familiar with the contrasts between *langue* and *parole*, synchrony and diachrony, signifier and signified. To the *Course in General Linguistics* has repeatedly been attributed, for example, the notion that the linguistic sign is arbitrary. Theorists with left-wing sympathies were inclined to regard this notion as revolutionary. If the relationship between the signifier and the signified is arbitrary and if we apprehend the world through language, then it appears that changes in language can effect changes in the world. Catherine Belsey said that "the sign is in an important sense arbitrary," "ideology is inscribed in ordinary language," and "it is in language that the ideology inscribed in language can be changed" (1980: 41, 43, 44). Terence Hawkes, too, claimed that the arbitrariness of language could mean "that reality remains genuinely ours to make and remake as we please" (1977: 21). Jacques Lacan even declared: "It is the world of words that creates the world of things" (1977: 65).[1] It became fashionable, accordingly, for critics to speak not of the *construing* (interpretation) of aspects of reality but, hyperbolically, of the linguistic and cultural *construction* of them, as in "constructions of identity" or "constructions of masculinity." The hyperbole is proportionate to the neglect of prior interpretable entities: if I contemplate a brick wall and say that I am "constructing" it, the bricklayer who built it may be understandably annoyed.

In a remarkably appropriate irony, the *Course in General Linguistics* which bears the name of Ferdinand de Saussure, proves, on close examination, to have been written not by Saussure at all but by eight of his students (mustering their old lecture-notes) and three editors. Saussure became famous for a work which he never saw and which, according to his editors, "he probably would not have authorized" (1961: xiii-xiv, xvi).[2] Few academics today, we may reflect, would relish the prospect of being commemorated posthumously by a work attributed to them but actually compiled from their students' lecture-notes. As a mark of respect for the real Ferdinand de Saussure, and in the interests of clarity and honesty, this essay hereafter refers to the collaborative team, the book's real authors, not as "Saussure" – as is regrettably customary – but as "Saucisse," a singular proper noun with appropriate degrees of similarity and difference.

Saucisse declares that the linguistic sign consists of just two things: the signifier, which is "auditory," being "*a slice of sound*," a "sound-image," and the signified, the associated "concept" (70, 104, 66). But what of the name "Ferdinand de Saussure" on the book's title page? It seems odd to refer to it as a "sound-image" if we are reading silently and not imagining its vocal utterance. But even if we do concede that it counts as a "sound-image," it initially evokes not a concept so much as a referent: we naturally assume that it refers to a real author, an actual

---

[1] Terry Eagleton has astutely commented that the "view of reality as essentially a product of language was simply the latest version of the classical idealist doctrine that the world was created by human consciousness" (1983: 108).

[2] Subsequent quotations from the text in English are from the 1959 translation (rpt. 1961). The original editors Bally and Sechehaye ask: "Will the critics be able to distinguish between the teacher and his interpreters?" One answer is that the critics have usually felt no need to do so.

Ferdinand de Saussure who wrote the book. We then learn, on reading the editors' "Preface to the First Edition," that this signifier on the title page is a liar. If the real Saussure "probably would not have authorized" the book, the link that the signifier makes with the referent is fraudulent.

Saucisse repeatedly claims that the linguistic sign consists merely of the sound-image plus the concept, and "not a thing and a name" (66), a claim which makes language seem curiously detached from reality. What is missing from his notion is, as I have indicated, the referent: an entity in the world to which the linguistic sign may refer. If I say to a friend, "This is your glass of beer, on the right," it is not enough for the friend to relate the sounds to mental concepts. Communication will be effective only if he relates my words to the correct referent, his glass of beer on the table. An even simpler example would be "Just look at that!" when I point to a burning house. The term "that" will have little conceptual content until the referent is seen. Terry Eagleton has offered an appropriately caustic comment on the *Course*: "In order to reveal the nature of language, [Saucisse] ... had first of all to repress or forget what it talked about: the referent, or real object which the sign denoted" (1983: 109).[3] Saucisse's failure to include the referent in his definition of the sign seems peculiarly obtuse, given that, from time to time, he cannot evade conceding its importance, and therefore veers into self-contradiction. He remarks, for example: "In zoology, the animal immediately presents itself. Astronomy works with units that are separated in space, the stars" (106-07).

Saucisse was also influentially imprecise in his use of tenses. Numerous readers have been misled by the present tense when he states: "The bond between the signifier and the signified is arbitrary ... I can simply say: '*the linguistic sign is arbitrary*'" (67; italics in original).[4] This use of the present tense gave readers the notion that language, in our era, is easily changeable. Unfortunately for them, what Saucisse evidently meant was that in some remotely primæval era, when primitive beings were first formulating language, a nominating procedure occurred: those beings conferred names on objects that did not naturally bear them: no tree

---

[3] I courteously substitute "Saucisse" for Eagleton's "Saussure."

[4] The tense is the same in the French text: "Le lieu unissant le signifiant au signifié est arbitraire ...[N]ous pouvons dire simplement: *le signe linguistique est arbitraire*" (1972: 100).

helpfully shouted "My name is 'tree!'" Saucisse should have used the past tense and said "the linguistic sign *was* arbitrary." This is confirmed when the *Course* claims that once a vocabulary becomes a language, a system accepted by a community, arbitrariness is replaced by the bonds of convention. Saucisse says:

> The signifier, though to all appearances freely chosen with respect to the idea that it represents, is fixed, not free, with respect to the linguistic community that uses it. The masses have no voice in the matter, and the signifier chosen by language could be replaced by no other ... No individual, even if he willed it, could modify in any way at all the choice that has been made; and what is more, the community itself cannot control so much as a single word; it is bound to the existing language. (71)

The theorists who saw revolutionary possibilities in Saucisse's work had not read it carefully, for it offered the conservative doctrine that, though language is conventional, those conventions soon become fixed – "the sign is unchangeable": "Of all social institutions, language is the least amenable to initiative. It blends with the life of society, and the latter, inert by nature, is a prime conservative force" (72, 74). Thus, although Saucisse's definition of the sign initially gives the false impression that language is highly malleable, his subsequent comments emphasise, and appear to exaggerate, the fixity of language as soon as a recognisable language has come into existence. His claim that the community "cannot control so much as an existing word" seems wrong. A community can, for example, declare that using certain terms in certain contexts is unlawful, or it can declare that a meeting's "Chairman" shall henceforth be its "Chairperson" or "Chair," while its "spokesman" becomes its "spokesperson." The *Course*'s fame demonstrates that a small community has influentially modified, if not controlled, the word "Saussure."

Furthermore, Saucisse's enthusiastic followers neglected the fact that the *Course* was repeating an ancient and rather obvious finding. In Plato's *Cratylus*, Hermogenes says: "I think no name belongs to any particular thing by nature, but only by the habit and custom of those who employ it and who established the usage" (1926 trans.; rpt. 1977: 11). Aristotle's *Organon*, too, had recognised the conventionality of language, so had St Thomas Aquinas, and so had Rabelais's Gargantua, who declares: "Utterances are meaningful not by their nature, but by choice" (all cited in Watson 1989: 49). Shakespeare's thirteen-year-old Juliet makes the point: "What's in a name? A rose, by any other name, would smell as sweet" (Watts, ed., 2000: II.ii.43-44).[5] Saucisse nevertheless asserts:

> in language there are only differences *without positive terms.* Whether we take the signified or the signifier, language has neither ideas nor sounds that existed before the linguistic system, but only conceptual and phonic differences that have issued from the system.[6] (120)

Thus, the word "cat" has meaning merely because it differs from "hat" and "mat." We may suspect, again, that the presence of real cats, hats, and mats in the world may have a bearing on the matter that Saucisse's formulation does not recognise. If there are no "positive terms" in language, it is difficult to see how, in the apparent absence of linguistic entities to differ, there could exist differences. The claim that no ideas or sounds existed before the linguistic system emerged seems obviously wrong, for if nobody had had the idea of (and the sounds for) giving names to entities in the world, no linguistic system would have come into existence. Even today, a person writing an essay is conscious of seeking words which will express adequately his or her prior – largely non-verbal – ideas.

Saucisse also declares:

> All our conventional values have the characteristic of not being confused with the tangible element which supports them. For instance, it is not the metal in a piece of money that fixes its value. A coin nominally worth five francs may contain less than half its worth of silver. Its value will vary according to the amount stamped upon it and according to its use inside or outside a political boundary. This is even more true of the linguistic signifier, which is not phonic but incorporeal – constituted not by its material substance but by the differences that separate its sound-image from all others. (118-19)

[5] Here, the phrase "any other name" (rather than "any other word") conforms to the First rather than the Second Quarto.

[6] Curiously, Saucisse's "sound-image" is "not phonic."

This promptly brings to mind the silver coin in Conrad's tale "Karain: A Memory." If, however, Saucisse had ever read "Karain," he might have felt obliged to rethink his *Course in General Linguistics.*

II

In "Karain," the eponymous hero, a Bugis chieftain, is haunted. Once, long ago, the sister of his friend Pata Matara had eloped with a Dutchman, a disgrace to the clan. For years, Karain and Matara had searched the East to find the lovers and take revenge. Karain, however, had become so obsessed by the beautiful image of the woman that eventually, instead of shooting the Dutchman, he had shot and killed Matara, in order to save her. Subsequently, Karain, possessed by guilt, has been haunted not by the woman's image but by the avenging spectre of Matara. The spectre has been kept at bay by Karain's sword-bearer, who supposedly wields supernatural powers and provides an efficacious charm. When the old sword-bearer dies, however, Karain finds that the ghost returns implacably to haunt him. In desperation, he turns to the British (apparently English) friends who have supplied him with guns and ammunition: Hollis, Jackson, and the anonymous narrator. Hollis produces a coin and, aided by his two colleagues, persuades Karain that it is an amulet with power to exorcise the ghost. (Captain Mundy, whose writings were a source for the story, says that the Bugis people of southern Celebes were not only deeply superstitious but also great admirers of the English: "They look to them for protection" [1848: I, 115, 82].) The device works: Karain, wearing what is termed "the infallible charm," is restored to confidence and peace of mind, even if it is not entirely certain that the cure will be permanent.

The narrator describes the coin thus: "It was a sixpence – a Jubilee sixpence. It was gilt; it had a hole punched near the rim." In my edition of the story, I have commented thus on the new coinage which appeared in the Jubilee Year of 1887:

> It included a silver sixpenny piece bearing the Queen's head on one side and the royal coat of arms on the other. Unfortunately, this coin, which was of relatively low value, had a close resemblance in size and design to the gold half-sovereign, which was of relatively high value; so it was often

> gilded in order to be fraudulently passed as the half-sovereign. In an appropriate irony, Hollis's "gilt" sixpence appears more valuable than it really is. (1990: 259)

There is more to be said on this topic. Both the silver sixpence and the gold half-sovereign were the same size, three-quarters of an inch (19 millimetres) in diameter, with milled edges. Both bore on one side, the obverse, the same image of Queen Victoria's head; while the other side, the reverse, bore (with small differences) a shield bearing the ensigns armorial of the United Kingdom. The wording differed somewhat, but it would obviously have been easy for someone to be fooled by a gilded version of the sixpence into thinking that it was the half-sovereign. As "Branch Manager" said in a letter to *The Times* of 22 June 1887:

> I think it a great blunder that the new sixpence should be precisely the same in size and pattern as the new half-sovereign and that it bears no indication of value. It will be very easy to gild these coins and pass them through banks for half-sovereigns where the amounts paid in are small. Where a credit consists of only a small amount of gold the cashiers simply count it without weighing. I think the sixpence should at once be withdrawn or the most cruel frauds will be perpetrated upon persons who will not be able to judge of the difference by feeling the weight, and the cashier's "short" will show a considerable increase. (cited in Lant 1973: 137-38)

By the end of November 1887, the Treasury arranged to replace the sixpence by one of a different design that specified its value. To give an idea of the value of each coin: in 1887 the price of a copy of *The Times* was three pence; so a sixpence would buy two copies, whereas a half-sovereign, worth ten shillings or 120 pence, would buy forty copies. (The nominal values would be equivalent, in the current British decimalised system, to 2½ pence and 50 pence, respectively.) Saucisse claims that a coin's value "will vary according to the amount stamped on it"; but neither coin had its value stamped on it. Prior decree and conventional acceptance, aided by the worth of the precious metal used, decided the monetary value, and that could, in turn, be falsified by disguising the metal's colour. Like the sixpence on which gilding disguises silver, the *Course in General Linguistics* has sought to magnify its value by employing the name "Saussure" to disguise its authorship by Saucisse.

Hollis's sixpence is doubly guilty: it is covered in gilt and guilt. (Conrad uses the ambiguous word "gilt" rather than the unambiguous "gilded.") The gilding, if perceived as such, reveals a fraudulent purpose. The Europeans pretend to Karain that the coin is an amulet with supernatural powers, when it is not; and, previously, someone endeavoured to present it as a gold half-sovereign, when it was not. Nevertheless, like a successfully fraudulent coin which purchases goods to its supposed rather than its real value, the "amulet" works: it does indeed banish Matara's ghost. The deception by the Europeans seems to be benign: certainly, it is intended as such. On the other hand, having been restored to his customary confidence and vigour as a local ruler, Karain will pursue a course that ultimately seems futile and may be self-destructive. The British group in the tale has been making money by illegally selling him arms. Karain uses these arms not merely to maintain his power in his small area of Mindanao but mainly to prepare for war against, we infer, the Spanish authorities in the region, and possibly also against the Dutch, so as to avenge the downfall of his mother's dynasty. His mother was "the ruler of a small semi-independent state on the sea-coast at the head of the Gulf of Boni" (48);[7] and we recall the historical facts that in the 1850s Base Kajuara, Queen of Boni, had "ordered her skippers to display the Dutch flag upside down on their ships" (Vlekke 1959: 299), and that the Dutch then retaliated with armed force, crushing the revolt of her people in a campaign during 1859-60. On 29 March 1860, *The Times* reported: "The people have submitted, the Queen has taken to flight, and her successor will hold office as a vassal of Holland" (11). These facts explain why Karain has made an odyssey so far from his homeland and harbours dreams of warfare. But warfare against the imperialist powers, in that region in the second half of the nineteenth century, would have been a futile struggle against superior force. He does not understand, we are told, "the irresistible nature of the forces which he desired to arrest." Near the end of the tale, Jackson remarks to the narrator: "I saw a paper this morning; they are fighting over there again. He's sure to be in it. He will make it hot for the caballeros. Well, good luck to him, poor devil!" (88).

---

[7] Because of the textual unreliability of Dent's Collected Edition, generally used for references in this journal, quotations from Conrad are from the editions cited below.

Jackson, as the word *caballeros* indicates, assumes that Karain will be fighting the Spanish. The moral situation of the group of Englishmen has certainly been ambiguous. By helping Karain, they have helped a picturesque chieftain whom they have come to regard as a friend. But their original motive was mercenary: they sold him arms to make a profit, and they cease the trade not because of moral compunction but because they risk arrest by the authorities: "the game was becoming at last too dangerous; and ... it was decided for us by some very respectable people sitting safely in counting-houses that the risks were too great" (53). In any case, they, Europeans, have been selling to a Bugis chieftain weaponry that could be used against other Europeans seeking to maintain law and order in the region. As so often in Conrad's works, loyalty is commingled with treachery. If Karain has been treacherous, so too have the Europeans been, whether individually (a person betraying a loved one or an ideal) or politically (illegally selling guns to be used against other Europeans and perhaps helping to bring about the death in battle of a friend).

When Karain, terrified by the spectre, had swum out to the Englishmen's vessel, he had claimed that white men "despise the invisible voices" and that the spectre pursuing him "cannot abide your unbelief" – "Oh! the strength of unbelievers!" Another sequence of ironies, however, is provided by Conrad's endeavours to erode the contrast between the "superstitious" Muslim and the "unbelieving" Europeans. One reason for the effectiveness of the amulet bearing the head of Queen Victoria is that Karain has long been fascinated by that monarch's fame and power:

> He ... inquired about the Queen. Every visit began with that inquiry; he was insatiable of details; he was fascinated by the holder of a sceptre the shadow of which, stretching from the westward over the earth and over the seas, passed far beyond his own hand's-breadth of conquered land. He multiplied questions; he could never know enough of the Monarch of whom he spoke with wonder and chivalrous respect – with a kind of affectionate awe! Afterwards, when we had learned that he was the son of a woman who had many years ago ruled a small Bugis state, we came to suspect that the memory of his mother (of whom he spoke with enthusiasm) mingled somehow in his mind with the image he tried to form for himself of the far-off Queen whom he called Great, Invincible,

> Pious, and Fortunate. We had to invent details at last to satisfy his craving curiosity; and our loyalty must be pardoned, for we tried to make them fit for his august and resplendent ideal. (46-47)

For Karain, then, the image on the coin helps to guarantee its power, and the image of the distant Great Queen is possibly mingled with recollections of his mother. The Englishmen have "had to invent details" to gratify him, magnifying Victoria as they later magnify the coin bearing her image. Here one irony is, of course, that as the reign of Queen Victoria proceeded through the decades, the monarch was increasingly eulogised in England as the "mother of her people," and, in the Golden Jubilee celebrations of 1887, the year of the commemorative sixpence, the demonstrations were not just patriotic but strongly centred on the revered figure of Victoria herself. The tale "Karain" was published in 1897, the year of her Diamond Jubilee, when imperialistic and royalist fervour reached even greater heights. Numerous readers of Conrad's tale at that time would have perceived the simple irony that Karain's naïve, superstitious reverence for Victoria was not so different from the reverence expressed and demonstrated by so many British people at both Jubilees.

When producing the sixpence, Hollis remarks: "A charm for our friend . . . The thing itself is of great power – money, you know – and the imagination is struck." The coin represents, among other things, the power of money in the world, and particularly the power of money in Great Britain. That power, in turn, rests partly on superstition, on faith, and on belief in a nation's wealth, stability, and future prospects. Next, Hollis says: "This is the image of the Great Queen, and the most powerful thing the white men know"; but now, tactfully, the "most powerful thing" becomes not money but the Queen's prestige: "She is more powerful than Suleiman the Wise, who commanded the genii," he tells Karain in Malay; then, speaking English, he tells his colleagues:

> "She commands a spirit, too – the spirit of her nation; a masterful, conscientious, unscrupulous, unconquerable devil . . . that does a lot of good – incidentally . . . a lot of good . . . at times – and wouldn't stand any fuss from the best ghost out for such a little thing as our friend's shot." (83-84)

Once again, the words erode the distinction between foreign superstition and domestic patriotism. Victoria is seen as controlling the turbulent, unruly, and "masterful" national spirit, a "devil" capable of mastering "the best ghost out." The imagery slides between the metaphoric and the literal. Incidentally, Hollis reminds us that, to some devout Muslims, the depiction of a human head (as on the sixpence) would seem offensively idolatrous, an affront to the Islamic aniconic tradition. Fortunately, Karain is not "very strict" in his faith.

Thus, as signifier, the coin by now has accumulated numerous "signifieds." If the gilding deceives Karain's eyes, he may take it to be gold. As the narrator sees the coin as a gilded sixpence, to him (and probably to his colleagues) it is a coin signifying, among many other things, a numismatic blunder and an envisaged fraud: evidence of British incompetence and dishonesty. Since Hollis's rhetoric persuades Karain, the little object signifies for the Muslim the supernatural power of the Queen's image to overcome the ghost that haunts him. But, to British observers, the coin and the image are reminders of their nation's wealth, economic and imperial power, and of the intangible spirit linking the regal image to imperial pride and prestige. If rhetoric has converted the coin into an efficacious talisman, rhetoric, too, may create a mystique of monarchy and empire.

The coin was produced from a box containing sentimental treasures: a cabinet photograph of a young woman, a bunch of flowers, a narrow white glove, a blue ribbon, and a packet of letters. The narrator comments: "Amulets of white men! Charms and talismans! Charms that keep them straight, that drive them crooked, that have the power to make a young man sigh, an old man smile ... Gifts of heaven – things of earth" (82). Once again, the tale strategically erodes the distinction between the exotic and the domestic. Europeans, too, may invest material objects with powerful significance. A picture, a glove, some letters: these may evoke memories of a love affair and exert continuing emotional force. In a rhetorical passage, the narrator imagines that for a moment (until the coin is produced), the schooner's cabin becomes filled with "the ghosts driven out of the unbelieving West": "all the exiled and charming shades of loved women; all the beautiful and tender ghosts of ideals, remembered, forgotten, cherished, execrated; all the cast-out and reproachful ghosts of friends admired, trusted, traduced, betrayed, left dead by the way" (82). The cabin seems "the only place of avenging belief" (83). If Karain seems primitive and superstitious in deeming that he is haunted by the avenging ghost of the friend he had betrayed, the Westerners, for all their supposed scepticism, are not so different: Europeans, too, may be haunted (if less intensely) by avenging memories of betrayed loved ones friends and ideals. "Every one of us ... you'll admit," says Hollis, "has been haunted by some woman" (81).

Certainly Hollis seems to be haunted by the memory of a woman he loved, but he makes the decision to mutilate a keepsake, a memento of her, for the sake of Karain. To make a container for the sixpence, he cuts a piece of leather from the palm of the glove, and, to suspend it from a neck, uses the blue ribbon from the box. He observes: "I shall make him a thing like those Italian peasants wear": Italian peasants wore amulets bearing an image of the Madonna, which could be made of gold, silver, or tin, on neck-chains. Conrad may also have known by this time (certainly he knew by the time of *Nostromo*) that South Americans sometimes wore an amulet in the form of a written prayer contained in a leather holder suspended from a rosary round the neck.[8]

In "Karain," the sixpence conveniently has a hole punched near the rim, indicating that it has already served as an ornament or amulet to be worn. As it was kept in Hollis's box of sentimental treasures, we may conjecture that it was once worn by a woman and/or was given to him by her to serve as a lucky token. Termed "a charm," it comes from a box that brings to mind "the charming shades" of young women. (Later, in "Heart of Darkness," Conrad will continue to play on the literal and metaphorical senses of "charm": Kurtz's African consort and his Intended have "powerless charms.") In cutting the glove, using the ribbon, and handing over the contained coin to Karain, Hollis may be regarded as symbolically placing the claims of male comradeship above the claims of his love of the woman. She, or at least her memory, becomes subordinate to the use as talisman of a female image on the coin. In attempting to exorcise a male ghost, Hollis may have exorcised a female one of his own. Karain had betrayed a bond between males, resulting in his breakdown; now, the breakdown is healed by a reassertion of male

---

8 Páez (1863: 54) refers to such an amulet as *La Oración del Justo Juez* ("The Prayer of the Just Judge"). In *Nostromo*, the emissary of Hernández accordingly refers to "the oration of the upright judge" (262, 434). Mario Curreli kindly provided the information about Italian amulets.

bonding. In this tale as in numerous other works, Conrad likes to use the classical term "shade," meaning "ghost of the dead," to refer to a recollected absent person, and the term erodes the distinction between the secular (if we take "shade" to be a poetic metaphor for the person as remembered) and the supernatural (since "shade" retains its ancient connotations). This repeated turn of phrase again blurs the distinction between the Europeans' world and Karain's.

The narrator does not specify the coin's inscription, but early readers would have known that on the obverse of the sixpence, the words surrounding the Queen's head are: "Victoria Dei Gratia Britt: Regina F. D.," abbreviating "Victoria Dei Gratia Britanniarum Fidei Defensor": in translation: "Victoria, by the Grace of God Queen of the British People and Defender of the Faith."[9] Ironically, the title "Fidei Defensor" was granted by Pope Leo X to King Henry VIII in recognition of his defence of Roman Catholicism. The faith defended by Victoria was, of course, the Protestant Christianity represented by the Anglican Church. Karain, as a devout Muslim, regards the British men as infidels, like all in their land: he refers to "your people, who live in unbelief; to whom day is day, and night is night – nothing more, because you understand all things seen, and despise all else!" (78). Yet he treats as an exception "the Great Queen" – "The Invincible, the Pious." So, when the coin is presented to him by the "infidels" as a talisman, the "Defender of the Faith" becomes a defender of a Muslim from an avenging spectre.

In a resourceful article which overlaps and anticipates some features of this one, David Adams (2001) has shrewdly pointed out a further irony that would have been evident to the tale's early readers. After the death of her husband, Prince Albert, in 1861, twenty-one years after her marriage to him, Queen Victoria entered a protracted phase of mourning, of which one illustration was that "for forty years, to the day of her death, she had fresh water delivered and clothes laid out in the bedchamber for her deceased prince" (738). The obsessive, perennial mourning of the black-clad Queen was highly conspicuous and widely noted; it even became a topic of criticism in the national press. Further-

---

[9] Its reverse bears the date, 1877, and the words "Honi Soit Qui Mal Y Pense" depicted on a garter. On the gold half-sovereign, the wording on the obverse is: "Victoria Dei Gratia"; on the reverse: "Britanniarum Regina Fid. Def." (with the date, 1887).

more, in 1870, William Rossetti, reflecting on the relationship between Victoria and John Brown, her devoted Scottish servant, alleged in his diary: "The real secret about John Brown and the Queen is that Brown is a powerful medium, through whom Prince Albert's spirit communicates with the Queen: hence Brown remains closeted with her alone sometimes for hours together" (cited in Weintraub 1987: 372). As Weintraub adds, "The period was one of intense interest in the occult." The image of Victoria helps to exorcise the shade haunting Karain, but Victoria remained haunted by the shade of her beloved consort.

The concluding passage of "Karain" is well known for its thematic adroitness. The narrator meets Jackson in the Strand in London. Jackson reflects that if the sixpence actually healed Karain, "never was a sixpence wasted to better advantage." He then wonders whether Karain was really haunted. The narrator, troubled, suggests that Jackson has been away from home too long, and, indicating the crowded, bustling street, says "Only look at this." There follows a bravura description which, while combining positive and negative features, predominantly emphasises the sheer reality of the city.[10] Jackson, however, is unconvinced: "I'll be hanged if it is yet as real to me as . . . as the other thing . . . say, Karain's story." The narrator concludes: "I think that, decidedly, he had been too long away from home." Eastern "superstition" has infiltrated the imagination of at least one of the British group; and the narrator's common sense may seem to resemble both a lack of imagination and a defensive resistance to the implications of his narrative.

One tiny part of that narrative, the gilt sixpence, has served as a multiple and richly ironic signifier. There is a comic disparity between the very small object and its very large burden of meaning. The silver coin was initially worth what it was called, sixpence; but the gilding has falsely sought to magnify its worth; and, having been defaced by the punched hole, a sign of its potential as a lucky charm, the sixpence is no longer legal tender, even if its silver retains some small monetary value as precious metal. It has signified the power of the monetary system, which is sustained largely by social faith. The images stamped on its surface function as signifiers of the monarchy, and particularly of a queen invested by many of her people with peculiar symbolic authority. The

[10] This crowd scene offers a symmetrical contrast to the depiction of the Eastern crowd, "brilliant, festive, and martial," in the second paragraph.

narrator does not quote the coin's inscriptions, but these would have been familiar to early readers, who would have handled such sixpences in everyday life. In part, the words signify the Queen's role as guardian of a particular religion. On the reverse, the inscription in French on a garter, "Honi Soit Qui Mal Y Pense" ("The shame be his who thinks evil of it"), evokes a legacy of British history that continued to Conrad's time and beyond. The Order of the Garter, established *circa* 1348, endures even in the 21st century. According to the best-known of the Order's etiological legends, Edward III picked up a blue garter which, at a ball, had embarrassingly fallen from the leg of a woman for whom he had great affection; he then gallantly tied it to his own leg as if it were a "favour" or love-token, while using the "Honi soit" admonition to assert his act's innocence.[11] Hollis, asking his companions to "lie a little" to make the best of the situation, publicly transfers love-tokens, souvenirs of a woman, to Karain.

The French in the coin's inscription is a reminder of the legacy of the Norman Conquest, while the Latin, evoking the power of the Roman Empire and its legacy of Latin to Europe, seeks to blend ancient Roman and modern British prestige. Layers of imperialism are linguistically encapsulated. To Karain the coin is an efficacious talisman, a magic charm produced by infidels to exorcise his ghost. It is efficacious partly because of his admiration for the Queen (associated with his mother) and partly because of the mumbo-jumbo (the rhetoric and dramatisation) employed by the Europeans when presenting it to him. Yet the mumbo-jumbo, as we have seen, tells its truths about the readiness of Europeans to mystify the monarchy and empire, and to be haunted by ghosts of their own. The Jubilee Year evoked by the sixpence was replete with rhetoric and dramatisation designed to glorify the Queen and her realms. Of course, the "healing" of Karain can be seen as an effective piece of psychotherapy aided by a little hypnotherapy,[12] but the use of the gilt coin is crucial. It denotes not only fraudulence but also real power, and it amply brings to mind the ways in which, in both the Eastern and the Western hemispheres, power may be sustained by story-telling, cheating, myths, faith, and superstition. If Hollis's rhetoric makes a damaged coin

---

[11] The legend is recounted in, for example, Selden 1631: 793.

[12] "They looked close into one another's eyes. Those of Karain stared in a lost glance, but Hollis's seemed to grow darker and looked out masterful and compelling" (84).

seem magical, he thereby resembles the Joseph Conrad who seeks to invest with magic the defaced currency of language: "the light of magic suggestiveness may be brought to play for an evanescent instant over the commonplace surface of words: the old, old words, worn thin, defaced by ages of careless usage" (xlix).

III

If Saucisse had read Conrad's tale carefully, he would have been able to refine his theory. He would have seen that a sign is not just a matter of "a slice of sound" and a concept, and that it is not necessarily fixed once a linguistic community has accepted it. He would have seen that the signifier may be visual and multiple, occasionally resembling a nest of boxes. He would have seen that what is signified may also be multiple and variable, sometimes directly and sometimes ironically related to its signifier; and that the signified may bear a shifting, complex relationship to a diversity of actual and possible referents which in turn generate significations. He might have speculated that the signified may become a signifier, and *vice versa*. The sixpence in "Karain" is shimmeringly protean in its values and meanings. If its financial value is low, it is nevertheless a treasure-house of implications; and its suggestions about language and meaning therefore constitute a rich complement to what we find in that overvalued book, so deceptively gilded with the name of Saussure, the *Course in General Linguistics*.

Works cited

Adams, David. "'Remorse and Power': Conrad's Karain and the Queen." *Modern Fiction Studies* 47.4 (2001): 723-52.

Belsey, Catherine. *Critical Practice.* London: Methuen, 1980.

Conrad, Joseph. *"Heart of Darkness" and Other Tales*, edited by Cedric Watts. Oxford: Oxford University Press, 1990.

——. Preface to *The Nigger of the "Narcissus,"* edited by Cedric Watts. London: Penguin, 1988.

——. *Nostromo*, edited by Cedric Watts. London: Dent-Orion, 1995.

Eagleton, Terry. *Literary Theory: An Introduction.* Oxford: Blackwell, 1983.

Hawkes, Terence. *Structuralism and Semiotics.* London: Methuen, 1977.

Lacan, Jacques. *Écrits*, translated by Alan Sheridan. London: Tavistock, 1977.

Lant, Jeffrey L. "The Jubilee Coinage of 1887." *British Numismatic Journal* 43 (1973): 132-41.

Mundy, Captain Rodney. *Narrative of Events in Borneo and Celebes.* 2 vols. London: Murray, 1848.

Páez, Ramón. *Wild Scenes in South America.* London: Sampson Low, Son, & Company, 1863.

Plato. *Cratylus, Parmenides, Greater Hippias, Lesser Hippias*, translated by H. N. Fowler. Loeb Classical Library. London: Heinemann, 1926, rpt. 1977.

Saussure, Ferdinand de. *Cours de linguistique générale.* 1916. Paris: Payot, 1972.

——. *Course in General Linguistics*, edited by Charles Bally and Albert Sechehaye in collaboration with Albert Reidlinger; translated by Wade Baskin. London: Peter Owen, 1959; rpt. 1961.

Selden, John. *Titles of Honour.* London: Richard Whitakers, 1631.

Shakespeare, William. *Romeo and Juliet*, edited by Cedric Watts. Ware: Wordsworth, 2000.

Vlekke, B. H. M. *Nusantara.* The Hague and Bandung: Van Hoeve, 1959.

Watson, George. *The Certainty of Literature.* Hemel Hempstead: Harvester Wheatsheaf, 1989.

Watts, Cedric. Explanatory Notes to *"Heart of Darkness" and Other Tales*, edited by Cedric Watts. Oxford: Oxford University Press, 1990.

Weintraub, Stanley. *Victoria: Biography of a Queen.* London: Unwin Hyman, 1987.

"Gaspar Ruiz": A Vitagraph of Desire

Sema Postacioglu-Banon
University of Venice Ca' Foscari

A SET OF SIX, regarded as Conrad's most varied collection of short serves in several ways as a bridge between *Nostromo* and the later novels. It can be located as a "suspension" in view of the quality of the stories that move towards yet unwritten, longer, far more complex novels. "The Informer" and "An Anarchist" are separate yet complementary nuclei to be reworked and incorporated in *The Secret Agent*, as "The Duel" and "Il Conde" will be in *Under Western Eyes* and *Victory*. In Robert Penn Warren's words, from his introduction to the Modern Library Edition of *Nostromo*, these later novels are "by and large, specializations and elaborations of elements that had been in suspension in that work" (cited in Guerard 1957: 216). At first sight, however, the forward thrust binding these stories together seems missing in "Gaspar Ruiz," which reaches backwards to the material of *Nostromo*. The short story with which the collection opens seems to unhinge itself from the stories that follow, and the "failure" of Conrad's plan to write another cycle of South American novels, similar to the Malay Lingard trilogy, centred on Gaspar Ruiz (or Benavides according to the story's literary source) does hint at the short story's resistance to be reworked as another piece of prose.

In a letter to H. G. Wells written in September 1908, Conrad expected "several additional centuries of Purgatory for that tale" (*CL4*: 128). The story, which by common consent reads like a thin adventure piece, has garnered little scholarly attention. Paul Kirschner (1964) has discussed Gaspar's futile attempt to satisfy his wife's demands against the story's main source. More recently, Mariano Siskind has argued that our difficulty in dealing with mixed identities and cultures may be related to academic interest in "the absolute otherness implied by Africa or South East Asia and the similarly absolute sameness embodied by Marlow" (2001: 54-55), and the relative lack of interest in South America. Although Siskind's critical remark deserves closer scrutiny because "hybrid" literary characters make heavier demands on the reader and call for equally complex treatment of cultural backgrounds, this essay does not take up the question of identity,[1] preferring to investigate whether the story's inverse movement is as regressive as it appears. The text, which seems to be regressive, uncoils as it leaps ahead to be penned again as the first film play of any notable literary quality in the 1920s, the period when cinema outgrew Sergei Eisenstein's notion of "montage of attractions" and could technically control a narrative line on screen, create cinematographic diegesis, and "harness visibility."[2] In addition, Conrad's often contradictory views on the theatre or film are not of interest here, and instead the focus is on the cinematographic narrative/ prose which, by chance or design, intersects with the new medium's growth.

Originally intended for publication in *Strand Magazine*, "Gaspar Ruiz" was serialized in the *Pall Mall Magazine* in July-October 1906. Conrad began writing the tale only a month after completing *Nostromo* in September 1904. The story stumbles out of the vast historical background of Sulacan society "ensconced behind its barriers" and turns its back on the Golfo Placido, without making its way as a piece of yet other "news from the interior" (*Nostromo* 37, 211). The events that take place in the story cannot be remedied, as Decoud cynically suggests, by another revolution. The shift to the Pacific coast and the narrated time shift to the liberation of Peru in the early nineteenth century open up a new geographical and figurative territory: the story places itself in that vast historical past and may have been an attempt to recuperate the very crux of Conrad's earlier work, his "broadest canvas," which consists in creating and writing history.

In the "Author's Note" to *Nostromo* (1918) and in a letter to Cunninghame Graham written in March 1923, Conrad claimed to have found "the seed" (Jean-Aubry, ed., 1927, 2: 299), the story's literary source, in Captain Basil Hall's *Journal of The Years 1820-21-22*. To this Norman Sherry adds John Miller's *Memoirs of General Miller in the Service of*

---

[1] Homi Bhabha explains that the concept of hybridity issues from "the strategy of disawoval" of a dominant authority, but the hybrid can unexpectedly challenge the rules of recognition of the same authority (1994: 110-11).

[2] Gunning 1990: 56. Harnessing narrative control on the screen also affected film production distribution. In 1915, The Motion Pictures Patents Company, whose largest producer, Vitagraph, was a member of, was declared illegal and supplanted by the first Holywood moguls.

the Republic of Peru (1829) as a second source (1971: 140-41). But the story's backbone is Gaspar's passion, which leads him to turn traitor and to become a national rebel and domestic hero, as Conrad grafts the fictional life of Gaspar Ruiz onto the land's historical chronicles:

> A revolutionary war raises many strange characters out of the obscurity which is the common lot of humble lives in an undisturbed state of society.
>
> Certain individualities grow into fame through their vices and their virtues, or simply by their actions, which may have a temporary importance; and then they become forgotten. The names of a few leaders alone survive the end of armed strife and are further preserved in history; so that, vanishing from men's active memories, they still exist in books. (3)

Contrary to what this opening suggests, the tale is slanted away from public historical leader figures. The opening introduces General Santierra, the historical figure who might have featured in the role of the hero in a conventional historical narrative; however, rather than being the story's protagonist, Santierra takes on the task of the *raconteur* of his memories and is an active witness of Gaspar Ruiz's story. Apart from a few digressions, his linear narrative adheres to the generic conventions of traditional historiography. The spear-headed progression of events discloses Ruiz's meandering adventures played in such a melodramatic key that it challenges not only our modern sensibility but also exasperates Santierra, after the earthquake episode, to the point of literally dismissing Gaspar:

> I had grown mistrustful of my interference. It had never been successful, and had not even appeared creditable. He was gone. Well, let him go. And he had carried off the Royalist girl! Nothing better. *Vaya con dios*. This was not the time to bother about a deserter who, justly or unjustly, ought to have been dead, and a girl for whom it would have been better to have never been born. (41)

Promptly, however, Gaspar makes his comeback by means of a letter whose wording suits Doña Erminia's vengeful spirit; he retrieves his good name and honour by raiding the Royalist troops and proving his worth to San Martin, the liberator of Peru and Chile (the "generalissimo," "His Excellency") and is appointed Captain of the Republican forces (45). As San Martin concedes, the audacity of his requests matches the degree of personal courage required in any revolutionary war. But the intimate and strictly private sphere keeps spilling over its confines and serves as a yardstick to assess public and political deeds. The man, whose life may be of interest only to himself, keeps bouncing into the foreground by unwittingly subverting the military hierarchy and its decisions. It can be argued that Gaspar is neither reflective nor capable of doubt and that his characteristic opacity might have made him invisible both to his superiors and the reader, but what pulls him and his story in opposite directions is the tension played out between Santierra and Doña Erminia. The story unfolds between these two irreconcilable poles and ends up politicizing a man initially devoid of political consciousness. This tension in Gaspar's previously "acquiescent soul" seals his fate and ironically substantiates the reference-free proverbs that Santierra utters at the beginning of Gaspar's story: "Every bullet has its billet," "Man discharges the piece, but God carries the bullet" (6, 18).

The real lever behind Gaspar Ruiz is Doña Erminia, whose old Spaniard father was ruined by the revolution but retained his political creed and passed on to his daughter his hatred and thirst for revenge against those fighting for independence from Spain. Her name in the diminutive suggests a kinship with Hermes, the mediator between the dead and the living, the old and the new. Her pull towards the past, her refusal to recognize the birth of a new society and nation, in short, a new epoch in history, is encapsulated in her pathetic remark "'We, too, have been left for dead – here'" (28). The pronouncement comes ironically just when Gaspar, rising from under the heap of corpses and with a bleeding wound, comes to her door for help and is expected to choose sides even before entering her house:

> "For the love of God," Gaspar Ruiz murmured.
>
> "Does not all the land belong to you patriots?" the voice on the other side of the door screamed on. "Are you a patriot?"
>
> Gaspar Ruiz did not know. "I am a wounded man," he said, apathetically. (21)

On the other hand, General Santierra represents the *criollo*, not a go-between between past and present but between the present and the future. As a *criollo,* his bond to a new national and cultural identity, which has nothing to do with fetishizing material gains extracted out of the bowels of this territory, is the sacred element, *la santa terra* or Santierra. In his discussion of *Nostromo*, Jacques Berthoud describes this type of "historical faith" as "commitment to the country for its own sake – inspired by personal emotion and sustained by individual assumptions about the nature of public events" (1978: 127). In the absence of such faith, Sulaco society with its grand scheme of "material interests" flounders. Santierra explains his own distinction more directly:

> I, of course, disregarded the noise of that madman [Emilia's father] with that feeling of superiority the success of our cause inspired in us Americans. I suppose I really despised him because he was an old Castilian, a Spaniard born, and a Royalist. Those were certainly no reasons to scorn a man; but for centuries Spaniards born had shown their contempt of us Americans, men as well descended as themselves, simply because we were what they called colonists. We had been kept in abasement and made to feel our inferiority in social intercourse. And now it was our turn. (23-24)

Once the new era takes its turn, though, it relies on no less violence than Spanish rule. Santierra, whose mother was French, "the daughter of an ardent republican" and who himself as a young boy "fought for liberty" because he "always believed in the equality of men," recalls Gaspar's story precisely because of his own "indignation" (26) at the brutality with which the Republicans treated their prisoners:

> The torment of my sensibility was so great that I wished the sergeant to fall dead at my feet, and the stupid soldiers who stared at me to turn into corpses; and even those wretches for whom my entreaties had procured a reprieve I wished dead also, because I could not face them without shame. … How long could it have been? A minute? If you measured by mental suffering it was like a hundred years; a longer time than all my life has been since. (11-12)

Santierra does admit that the sweeping ideals of revolution can dangerously boil down to ruthlessness and cruelty; the men fighting for equality, such as General Robles, can easily become tyrants themselves. But standing firmly on the historical winners' side, Santierra neither allows this insight to shake his political convictions nor wishes to revise the past. A revolutionary war, he says, does not leave the enemy without "but within your very house" (24). No matter how destructive and "shocking" the revolution turns out to be, Santierra notes this turn of events with "a glance in the direction of the murmur," concluding serenely: "'Yes. That is, war – calamity'" (25).

Interestingly, Santierra's straightforward and even reductive view of history seems to accord, uncharacteristically, with that of the author. For once in his literary career, Conrad seems to side with revolution and revolutionaries – a quite unconscious slip that the later novels *The Arrow of Gold* (1919) and *The Rover* (1923) attempt to remedy. To Santierra, men *are* brothers *not* because of their mutual love or care for each other, but because of their "fierce animosity" and their need to "display their differences": "There is no doubt to their brotherhood ... All men are brothers, and as such know almost too much of each other" (26). Much earlier, without the benefit of Santierra's wisdom in old age, Conrad put it with greater vigour to Cunninghame Graham on 8 February 1899: "What does fraternity mean. Abnegation – self-sacrifice means something. Fraternity means nothing unless the Cain-Abel business. Thats [*sic*] your true fraternity" (*CL2*: 159).

As seen through Santierra's panoramic historical perspective of the winner, fratricidal strife lessens the impact of the story's ever-increasing violence. The tale's peculiarly "grotesque" quality consists in the unrestrained expression of violence. This ushers in the film-like or cinematographic quality of "Gaspar Ruiz," for the tale comes as a "race across the disintegrating ice of narrative continuity" (Coates 1983: 20) long before being rewritten for the screen. History and Santierra's position as a winner provide the surface, the screen upon which natural and man-made catastrophes glide. Even the earthquake that devastates towns and villages, killing Erminia's parents, and thus uniting Gaspar and Erminia, or with much irony "levelling their distinctions" (37), is in retrospect reduced to negligibility.

It may help to recall, by way of comparison, Heinrich von Kleist's masterpiece *Das Erdbeben in Chile* [The Earthquake in Chile], published in 1807. Set in 1647, at the time of the great earthquake in the "Kingdom of Chile," this is the tragic love story between a young Spanish tutor, Jeronimo Rugera, and Josepha, the only daughter of the nobleman Don Henrico Asteron of Santiago. The entire tale is singularly burdened with untold and unspoken indirect rules and obligations. The social hierarchy transferred to the old Spanish community in the New World is the ruling order. But once the young people trespass that order's boundaries, Josepha is sent to a Carmelite convent and Jeronimo to prison. When an earthquake occurs, it devastates the entire town, its prison, its guillotine, the Viceroy's palace, and the tribunal, eventually freeing the young lovers. But what looks like nature's victory is in the end suppressed by a religious fanaticism that exceeds even nature's destructive-liberating power, as the story ends with the lynching of the lovers.

A century before Conrad, an earthquake could serve as the pivotal point of a tale, in that it frees the lovers and allows them to be reunited however temporarily. Kleist, the great outsider on the fringe of Romanticism and German classicism, is, as Stefan Zweig observed, the pre-modern voice quarreling with vertical authority. In "Gaspar Ruiz," however, the earthquake's significance – as that of firing squads and torture – is thinned out and made slippery, no longer capable of forming a narrative centre that would serve either to reconcile or polarize human historical destructive powers.

Despite the onrush of Gaspar's adventures, there are several suggestions in the story of a mythopoeic wish for a renewed Saturnian Age and a return to epic narrative. For instance, Gaspar's and Doña Erminia's orphaned daughter, whose face is less wan and haughty than her mother's, still has the same eyes, eyes that resemble Moneta's, the Goddess of Memory and Mother of the Muses. The name Moneta, "admonisher" in Latin, does fit the younger Erminia, Santierra's "guardian angel," insofar as she admonishes the old general by shaking her finger at him while taking leave of the curious onlookers and of the story. But this is only a fleeting suggestion of an epic quality that never materializes and is even turned into farce when Santierra's English seamen guests flatly observe that she is, after all, a "short, stout, old girl" (69).

Even more obviously, there is the motif of Gaspar's titanic strength, the story's pivot. Prison bars yield to his grasp, which he bends only to reach for buckets of water. He tolerates immense hardship and physical suffering; he keeps fighting until his last breath – yet strength and "strong clay" do not suffice. On the contrary, titanic might proves to be the very weakness of a man incapable of assessing the demands placed on him. It is true that he first makes a choice by joining the Republicans, later finds himself fighting for the Royalists, and once rescued by his future wife, turns into a faithful husband and unflinchingly chooses to serve a desperately regressive force. When he tells her "You are my strength," he literally transfers to her not only the might of his limbs but also the power and capacity to formulate his inarticulate "sluggish anger" (39, 5). Despite Santierra's reconciliatory but not altogether forgiving look at Gaspar's personal and the national past, Gaspar's turbulent life stretches on the tense opposition between forces that never coalesce.

The mythopoeic elements, furthermore, are barely detectable "bumps." They neither develop into a force strong enough to open a fissure nor do they constitute a challenge to the narrative premises. Only once does Santierra seem to question these, which he does to tell his story of "a dreadful amazement which the further experience of life, of more than fifty years, has done nothing to diminish" (25). However, after solidifying Santierra's own cause and historical stance, Gaspar is reduced to a spectacle, which in turn places the reader in the position of a spectator. The scant critical interest the story has aroused could perhaps be due to Conrad's insistent spectacularization.

In a 1923 letter to Cunninghame Graham, Conrad appropriately recalls "And now the very writing of it seems like the memory of a *dream*!" (Jean-Aubry, ed., 1927, 2: 300; emphasis added). In dreams, Freud tells us, we do not hear words but see pictures. Conrad also admitted to having to invent "the scenery" for his source and to fleshing out his story visually. The narrative perspective that sweepingly takes in the historical events calls for rapid change, which implies movement and action but no reflection. There is, indeed, too little left for the reader's inner to probe the text. It is the function of the inner eye and its engagement, Leon Edel points out, that make the major distinction between the textual narrative and cinema: a camera "asks nothing of our mind's eye. It is all there for us to see, not to imagine; it is only the eye, rarely the mind's eye, that must be quick, and there is almost too much for it to take in" (1974: 183). In the short story, Santierra is the narrative perspective and the camera, although it is certainly a fixed camera in terms of value judgements. The manner in which he recounts his memories goes far beyond Conrad's artistic credo, which summarizes modernity's ocularcentrism: "to make you see," that is, "seeing" in terms of understanding and imagining. Santierra's narrative attempts to "move" pictures. Once he makes his point clear, the narrative drowns in lavish scenes of action and comes too close to the visual appeal of chase films, "the original truly narrative genre of the cinema providing a model for causality and linearity as well as a basic editing continuity" (Gunning 1990: 60). It is no coincidence that Conrad picked this story of South America to rewrite for the screen – a potential counterpart to the American epic narrative of D. W. Griffith's *Birth of A Nation* (1915), shot without a written scenario, but whose technical innovations served to organize and codify narrative unity and topographical complexity on film.[3]

Conrad may not have been sure about how to proceed with writing for the screen, and may have received help from his agent Pinker; but as Gene M. Moore carefully argues, Pinker's presence need not mean that outright collaboration occurred (1997: 36-37). Despite Conrad's limited knowledge of the new media, major credit for the screen adaptation should go to Conrad's experience of adaptation: "To-morrow" as *One Day More* (1904) and *The Secret Agent* as a four-act play (1919). In a letter to Thomas J. Wise of 1 November 1920, Conrad admits that his rewriting consisted in "a consecutive development of the story in a series of descriptions, just as the whole thing presented itself to me when I first began to think the subject out in its purely visual aspect" (Jean-Aubry, ed., 1927, 2: 250). More significantly, Conrad wrote to Eric Pinker: "I with the book before me suggested the wording depicting the episodes from the film point of view" (31 January 1923; cited in Moore 1997: 36).

This gives a fairly good picture of Conrad re-reading his "Romantic Tale." What emerges from this media-transposition is consequently, first, Conrad's own response as a reader to his story; this response then re-shapes the narrative perspective and lends especially to Gaspar quite articulate loquacity achieved with the help of inter-titles and dialogue titles. This may be all the more interesting because the original tale's tongue-tied protagonist becomes audible in a script for a silent film.[4]

---

[3] In a letter to Pinker of 1915, Conrad writes that "it was Jessie's idea" to adopt the story for the screen (*CL*5: 497).

[4] H. G. Wells, who had earlier found fault with Conrad's flow of words, proved to have a far vaguer idea of film-making when he wrote his first film script *Things to Come* (1936) based on *The Shape of Things to Come* (1933). Wells's script had virtually no dialogue, and Wells believed that films could be crafted single-

The screenplay follows the original story quite closely in its sequence of events but brings a significant change to the narrative perspective. Its main interest lies in Conrad's engagement with what looks like a mere "technicality" and in the manner in which an altogether new media perspective affects the writing.

To begin with, the film play lacks a frame-narrator. The removal of this narrator does not mean that Santierra is automatically left as the single narrator. Conrad's potential script with its elaborate stage directions is penned with the perfect awareness of directing a camera whose vision does not correspond to Santierra's. Furthermore, the demands Conrad puts on his authorial camera to tell an essentially subjective story appear far ahead of their time. In around 1920, the so-called "transitional cinema" recently completed its course from one-reel to feature films based on a narrative and saw the emergence of a new mode of editing "character subjectivity." This mode consisted in "the point-of-view shot," that is, the cut from a character to what the character sees and then back to the character (Pearson 1996: 31). Conrad's script abounds in such cuts, particularly when Gaspar is caught between two sides, as when a rifle is thrust into his hands or even earlier when he points to his own parents what he sees. Conrad need not have known what the current cinematography could accomplish, but he sensitively projects Santierra onto the screen by incorporating his vision and story within the camera eye/lens in order to tell Gaspar's tragedy. In the film play, Santierra does not only observe but is also being observed. "The Prologue Picture" creates the necessary encounter of the perspectives between the diegetic narrator and the authorial camera.

The opening scene at Santierra's stately house in Valparaiso initially stresses the time of narration and the narrated time, 1850 and 1830, respectively. Conrad relies on décor and costumes to convey the temporal split at the lunch the General offers to his English guests. It is the young servants and the English seamen of unspecified rank who move, mime talk, and fill the space between the potential audience sitting before the screen and the silent, immobile trio, who make up the diegetic

handedly like novels. Raymond Massey, the actor who played the two central roles, commented in his autobiography: "The picture was fantastically difficult to act . . .Wells had deliberately formalised the dialogue . . .We were always the puppets of Wells, completely under his control" (quoted in Frayling 1995: 20-22).

audience on screen: the elderly Santierra at the head of the table, the captain on one side, and the major-domo at Santierra's back. The young and the elderly form a hierarchical symmetry as an initial "tableau"; this static portrayal provides the frame for the story line to start uncoiling. Its movement occurs in the space Conrad negotiates between the audiences noted above. For although the stripes and badges on the sailors' costumes are intended to mark differences of rank and age, the stress of the (potential) camera falls on those parts of the body that clothes do not cover: first, the bare feet of the servants on the floor; then, the biceps of an English seaman on the table; and, lastly, Santierra's eyes, which look up towards his own portrait as a young officer hanging on the wall. When joined together, such a progression presents a curve moving upwards and away from the audiences. Its ending marks the moment when Gaspar's story resurfaces in Santierra's memory following the theatrical jocular display of a sailor's strength. Remembering induces silence among the "low" and "young." The guests stop joking and turn their heads to Santierra. All eyes look in the same direction. Just when the authorial camera focuses on Santierra's upturned eyes, it also absorbs them and from this instance onwards Gaspar's story can unfold. As in the short story, the source of Gaspar's narrative remains Santierra's memory; at intervals reference is also made to the prologue scene to remind spectators of the film story's "reality." On the surface, the film play seems to follow the short story's episodes and events, but after Conrad's camera "swallows" the historical protagonist's eye, can it still be telling the same story?

In his speech "Author and Cinematograph," delivered during his spring 1923 visit to America, Conrad makes a significant comparison between the author and the camera:

> Long before the idea occurred to scientists and means devised by technicians that sun can make pictures, at first motionless and afterwards moving, the aim of the novelist has been (at least one of his aims) to present humanity in action on the background of the changing aspects of nature and a series of acted scenes exhibiting part of life in a connected series up to some appointed conclusion. *But the author unlike the camera had the power to react not only to light, shades and colour but also to form.*
> (cited in Schwab 1965: 345; emphasis added)

What does the film play try to articulate, and how does its broader perspective shape what Santierra recalls?

"The Prologue Picture" moves swiftly from jokes and riddles to the core story and concludes with a biblical reference. Gaspar, in Santierra's words, is "a Samson" (MS 3/TS 3).[5] To Gaspar's remarkable build and an equally big head there is the added "shock ... of hair falling on his shoulders," the hidden seat of Samson's supernatural strength (MS 4, 44 / TS 3, 20; Judges: 17-22). Moreover, similar to the story of Samson, Gaspar's erotic desire from the very beginning shapes his master-slave relationship with Erminia. Unlike Samson, however, Gaspar displays no courage to demand the woman of his desire; his timidity and restraint before her implies that she must be beyond his reach. This consequently alters how they get to know one another. From the very beginning Gaspar and Erminia are no strangers. Erminia is not simply the daughter of some unnamed fallen Royalist family dwelling in a remote place, who Gaspar incidentally encounters and who heals his wounds. She is "the daughter of our master," Gaspar announces to his parents (MS 4/TS 3). Interestingly, this is no mystery to the Republicans who loot and burn Gaspar's house: "He looks like a quiet chap. We will make him a soldier of Liberty . . . And that was your master's daughter, eh?" (MS 8/TS 5).

Erminia's father, an "ex-member of the ex-viceroy's council," is called Don Carlos Ximenes (MS 9/TS 5), a name that emphasizes his aristocratic origins. The first time Erminia is seen while riding a horse, Gaspar rescues her from being crushed by a falling tree and he later saves her from the Republican troops. Arrogantly but expectedly, she does not thank him but merely condescends to look down on him. Gaspar, by contrast, lowers his head, and when Erminia later touches his wound, "he is moved to inward rapture" (MS 27/TS 13). Presenting Gaspar and Erminia as acquaintances set apart by a solid class divide does effect Gaspar's apparent "neutrality" at the height of a civil war. Is he still the man who could neither understand heroism nor see no reason "to uphold in his own person the rule of the King of Spain" (6)?

Although we see him fighting first with the Revolutionaries and then with the Royalists, Gaspar no longer seems to waver between

---

[5] Joseph Conrad, *Gaspar The Strong Man: Scenario of a Film Play*, unpublished. Quotations from the script indicate both the manuscript (Yale University) and typescript (Colgate University) page numbers.

historically opposite poles. More significantly, the film play omits the historical conflict's background. The Republicans and Royalists are there, but why they are fighting is obscure. The original story's tension is lacking: gone are the humiliation the Republicans (colonists) have suffered from the Royalists and Santierra's shame at the terror brought about by his own Republican comrades. Because the script glosses over the short story's essential dynamics, the Republicans, the freedom fighters, first appear to be no better than vandals without a cause. For instance, the Republicans' angry cry heard while raiding hamlets – "All those Royalists shall be made beggars. But people like you are their dogs and I shall burn your kennel . . . Liberty or death!" (MS 8/TS 5) – presents the Royalists as victims. Seen in this light, the Independence War risks becoming just another in a series of unending military conflicts. (In the short story, by contrast, Santierra's firm historical perspective prevents precisely this from happening.) If, in the film play, no political faction is better qualified than another, why choose sides at all? Gaspar, however meek and quiet, knows where he wants to belong, simply crouching at Erminia's door as a faithful servant while Erminia towers above him. If occasionally he manages to stand upright as her equal, he never the less always capitulates in the end.

The civil war or the fratricidal strife fails to serve as the fulcrum in the film play because of the voracious appetite of Conrad's camera. Reduced to a historical fact in the background, the fighting in the film play need not have a rationale, and the war qualifies only as "a bountiful supply" for heroic deeds. This is also the point where the film play severs its bonds with its original: the narrative fluidity gained by Santierra's sense of history, which paves the way for the screen adaptation, takes a further leap by refusing to look back at its source. While the war provides the framework for melodrama, it never the less serves to present Gaspar's "desire" as heroic and to provide insights into his private life. Irreconcilable opposites, the film play seems to suggest, are no longer brothers at war, but housed in Gaspar's internal divisions. His drama is that of a man who unexpectedly becomes the "equal" of his master's daughter. Observing their odd union, Santierra remarks: "But that the proud and beautiful Dona Erminia, the admired of all at the Viceroy's receptions only a few months ago, would take by the hand a simple peasant, I would not have believed!" (MS 26/TS 13).

If an onlooker alone is left wondering at the sudden turn of events, could Erminia and Gaspar be expected to view their union simply as a matter of fact? Erminia's "Delilah-like" delicacy consists not only in her astuteness at bending Gaspar to her will but also in her ability to disguise her sense of incredulity. Although she never displays her own wonder, the controversy at the bottom of her demands becomes more marked on the screen by removing the War of Independence to the background. The same controversy also emphasizes her reluctance to accept the fortuitous union with Gaspar. From the very beginning the idea of making Gaspar rise in the Republican army is Erminia's. In Scene III, she even dictates to him the letter in which he asks the Republicans to restore his reputation. As a fallen court lady, Erminia knows that a good name rests on fidelity and a sense of duty, but just when the Republicans accept Gaspar as "their man" after his victory over the Spanish officers, she regrets this and "veils her eyes": "You were merciful to the soldiers of the King?" (MS 45/TS 21).

Does she realize only belatedly that she should not have tried to gain "recognition" for Gaspar from her own enemies? Why does her Royalist allegiance get in her way to accept Gaspar as an officer with restored honour? When she decides to recall and abide by her political faith inevitably coincides with Gaspar's military ascent, as though Gaspar's rise could substantiate their "equality" brought about forcefully by the revolution. Appropriately, Gaspar's military rise and wedding ceremony, both performed with equal pomp, are presented successively in the same scene (Scene IV). No sooner does Gaspar earn his "alienating" military title – "Do not ask me about the Señorita, for I prefer not to think of her when I am amongst you" (MS 44/TS 21) – than the humble "captain" of peasant stock, a *guasso*, takes great offence when none of his fellow officers show up at his wedding: "Not one officer in the church! What a slight! ... Is there no justice in this world? ... What is there for a man like me to trust?" (MS 47/TS 22).

At Erminia's suggestion "your strength," he raids the Governor's palace, gives up his military rank then and there, and becomes a guerilla leader. This last stage is actually a retreat to his *guasso* life – his initial point of departure – and completes a cycle. Inside "Gaspar's secret house" in a mountain gorge, Erminia's trajectory also closes off in a cycle. On home ground, she is seen once only – at childbirth. She has little to do with domestic affairs but belongs to the public arena; like a queen seated in her "sumptuous chair," she conducts ceremonies under the Spanish flag and, ever inaccessible, leaves the gorge only as a political hostage. Gaspar, by contrast, retreats from the war as it rages around him. First, as an affectionate father, he is seen singing and playing the guitar. Later, with Santierra imprisoned in Gaspar's military headquarters, the guerilla leader and his captive while away the time playing cards! Mentally, Gaspar dismisses the war he ought to be leading. In the end, neither his slackened vigilance nor his incapacity to detect danger brings about his death but his willingness to turn deaf and blind to the time he lives in.

The expression of this longing is the film play's strength. Unlike a film made in the shadow of a book, the film play attempts to respond to the shadow discarded in the short story by Santierra's misogyny. It articulates Gaspar's atavistic desire against the background of an insurmountable class divide and adds a more convincing and more realistic element to the mere unfolding of history. The knowledge that Gaspar's and Erminia's dilemmas issue from their inner conflicts diminishes the bland melodrama of "The Romantic Tale" and ultimately brings only the film play closer to the reconciliatory nature of film production. As Paul Coates notes, cinema, "whose powerful totalisations overwhelm the self," tends to reconcile individual and collectivity "by creating through art the illusion of reality" (1986: 3).

Acknowledgements

A version of this paper was presented at the Conrad and Territoriality Conference held at the University of British Columbia, Vancouver, in August 2002 in conjunction with the Joseph Conrad Society of America and with financial support from the Social Sciences and Humanities Research Council of Canada.

Quotations from *Gaspar The Strong Man: Scenario of a Film Play* appear by the kind permission of the Estate of Joseph Conrad. I am grateful to Carl Peterson for allowing access to copies of the film play.

Works cited

Berthoud, Jacques. *Joseph Conrad: The Major Phase.* Cambridge: Cambridge University Press, 1978.

Bhabha, Homi K. *The Location of Culture.* London: Routledge, 1994.

Coates, Paul. *The Realist Fantasy: Fiction and Reality since "Clarissa."* London: Macmillan, 1983.

———. *Words After Speech: A Comparative Study of Romanticism and Symbolism.* London: Macmillan, 1986.

Edel, Leon. "Novel and Camera." In *The Theory of The Novel: New Essays*, edited by John Halperin. 177-88. New York: Oxford University Press, 1974.

Frayling, Christopher. *Things to Come.* London: BFI Film Classics, 1995.

Guerard, Albert J. *Conrad the Novelist.* Cambridge, MA: Harvard University Press, 1957.

Gunning, Tom. "The Cinema of Attractions: Early Film, Its Spectator and the Avant-Garde." In *Early Cinema: Space, Frame and Narrative*, edited by Thomas Elsaesser and Adam Barker. 56-62. London: British Film Institute, 1990.

Jean-Aubry, G., ed. *Joseph Conrad: Life and Letters.* 2 vols. London: Heinemann, 1927.

Kirschner, Paul. "Conrad's Strong Man." *Modern Fiction Studies*, 10 (1964): 31-36.

Moore, Gene M. "Conrad's "Film-Play" *Gaspar the Strong Man.*" In *Conrad on Film*, edited by Gene M. Moore. 31-47. Cambridge: Cambridge University Press, 1997.

Pearson, Roberta. "Transitional Cinema." In *The Oxford History of World Cinema*, edited by Geoffrey Nowell-Smith. 23-42. Oxford: Oxford University Press, 1996.

Schwab, Arnold T. "Conrad's American Speeches and His Reading from *Victory.*" *Modern Philology*, 62 (1965): 342-47.

Sherry, Norman. *Conrad's Western World.* Cambridge: Cambridge University Press, 1971.

Siskind, Mariano. "Images of South America in Some Texts of Joseph Conrad." *Conradiana*, 33.1 (2001): 49-58.

Zweig, Stefan. *Der Kampf mit dem Dämon: Hölderlin, Kleist, Nietzsche* 1925; rpt. Frankfurt am Main: S. Fischer Verlag, 1951.

The Anarchy of Love: "The Informer"

P. A. March-Russell
University of Kent, Canterbury

> Cold reason, he boasted, was the basis of his optimism.
> *The Secret Agent* (1907)

> [...] the deadliest conflicts of the world are carried on in every breast capable of feeling and passion.
> "An Anarchist" (1906)

"THE INFORMER" (1906) is one of a number of Conrad's stories that has enjoyed fresh attention from scholars in recent years. In particular, Keith Carabine (1999) has shown how "the moral satirical idea" is central to understanding the text. This essay, in part, responds to Carabine's fine account in order to develop how Conrad's satire not only critiques the moral disaffection of its protagonists but also takes on the romantic form itself. My aim is to show how the combination of a multiple frame-narratives with unreliable narrators infers not only a tale within a tale but also a love story that, in its futility and human complexity, describes a range and depth of emotion that outstrips conventional romance. Furthermore, in suggesting a comparison between the story and Jacques Derrida's ethics of friendship,[1] I argue that the doomed love of Sevrin and the Lady Amateur is a genuinely anarchistic gesture since it describes a utopian desire that exceeds (and defeats) the comprehension of the anarchist-aesthetes. The very utopianism of this love is heightened by the extent to which it is inexpertly suppressed through the frame-

---

[1] In this respect, my article also contributes to the recent exploration of Conrad's writing in terms of post-modern ethics. See, for example, Gibson 1998.

narrative. Whereas the frame-narrators base their rationality upon an optimistic faith in the future, Sevrin's pessimistic (and therefore realistic) denial of redemption expresses a passion otherwise calculated away by the frame-narrators. In developing my argument, I suggest, first, how other critics have viewed the story, briefly consider the publishing context as a determinant on the text and, lastly, attempt to show how Conrad's use of the sentimental produces a fiction that is anything but anodyne.

Once considered a "pot-boiler" (Graver 1969: 144; Scanlan 1995: 115), "The Informer" is now numbered among, in Daphna Erdinast-Vulcan's terms, his "strange short fiction": tales that resist the resolution of the well-made story and interrupt, or estrange, the reader's consumption of the text. Despite this change in critical status, "The Informer" would, at first sight, seem to be unpromising material for such a reassessment. The romantic story – the elaborate unmasking of a police informer, Sevrin, within an anarchist cell because of his (fatal) love for a female member of it – complements the fiction in its original place of publication, the mainstream American journal, *Harper's Monthly Magazine*. The roles of romance, intrigue, and crime would have appealed to the sensibility of *Harper's* readers, as indicated by the text's publication under the dramatic sounding "The Informer" despite Conrad's preference for the more ambiguous and impressionistic title "Gestures" (*CL*3: 305).

Allied to the story's formulaic content are the circumstances of its composition. Like its companion-piece, "An Anarchist," also published in *Harper's*, the story was written to alleviate the debts that Conrad had accumulated during the protracted writing of *Nostromo* (1904). As he wrote to his literary agent, J. B. Pinker, on 12 May 1905: "short stories – is the watchword now" (*CL*3: 243). The high financial returns of magazine publication and the comparative speed with which a short story could be written, as opposed to the writing of a longer or more complex narrative, were strong motivations. In practice, though, the process proved agonizing: "What cuts me to the quick is the forced deterioration of my work produced hastily, carelessly in a temper of desperation" (*CL*3: 300). Conrad's self-criticism, compounded by the reasons for writing the stories and their place of publication, encouraged the critical view that these were either minor works or, at best, preparations for *The Secret Agent* (1907).

From the evidence of his letters, though, Conrad approached the design of "The Informer" as meticulously as his major fiction. Much of his discontent can, therefore, be attributed to his frustration at his artistic ideals being compromised by the financial and material pressures under which the text was written. Although the content is formulaic, the story's presentation is not. The narrative is told by an anonymous first-person narrator, a collector "of Chinese bronzes and porcelain" (73), who is introduced to the "revolutionary writer" (74) and secret anarchist, Mr X, through a fellow-collector. Mr X tells the uncomprehending frame-narrator the story of Sevrin and how he exposed Sevrin's betrayal.

As elsewhere in Conrad's short fiction, when the framing of the text is taken into account, the ironic effect achieved undercuts the seemingly simple narrative. In "The Informer," the effect is doubly ironic since Sevrin is tricked – or framed – into giving himself away. The act of framing is integrated as part of the story so that the frame-narrative is not only foregrounded but also interrogated. This discrepancy in terms of representation is further highlighted by the appended coda in which the narrator meets the Parisian friend who first introduced him to Mr X. The friend enthuses over Mr X's uniqueness to the aggravation of the narrator's "finer feelings," who replies "that the man's cynicism was simply abominable" (101). The companion agrees but then states:

> "And then, you know, he likes to have his little joke sometimes," he added in a confidential tone.
>
> I fail to understand the connection of this last remark. I have been utterly unable to discover where in all this the joke comes in. (102)

This last, enigmatic remark, capping an already ironic narrative style, has provoked much of the debate surrounding the story. As with other deliberate teases, such as Henry James's "The Figure in the Carpet" (1896) or Rudyard Kipling's "Mrs Bathurst" (1904), critics have sought to explain the joke's meaning even though its existence depends solely on the anonymous friend who arranges (and thereby frames) the narrator's encounter with Mr X. Earlier critics, such as James Walton and Allan Hepburn, assume the joke's presence as a given and view the narrator's incomprehension as the extent to which "he has been taken in, or collected by X" (Hepburn 1992: 109).

In emphasizing Mr X's duping of the narrator with a melodramatic tale about the criminal underworld, this interpretation sees the story as a critique of the *bourgeoisie* or, in Mr X's own words, "an idle and selfish class [that] loves to see mischief being made, even if it is made at its own expense" (78). Evidence for this reading can be found in that the narrator is proud to know, with regards to Mr X's political activism, "as a certainty what the guardians of social order in Europe had at most only suspected." In that sense, the narrator is implicated in Mr X's own demand for intrigue and secret knowledge: of being more aware and more included in the inner meaning of events than his fellow man. The narrator finds it "too frightful to think of" that Mr X could almost be his *Doppelgänger*: "he had the manner of good society, wore a coat and hat like mine, and had pretty near the same taste in cooking" (76). But both men position themselves against the ignorance of the majority, specifically the "amateurism" of those who dabble in interests – anarchism and aestheticism – of which they are connoisseurs.

Despite his protestations about Mr X's cynicism, the narrator admits to being impressed by his insight into social behaviour: "a demagogue has only to shout loud enough and long enough to find some backing in the very class he is shouting at" (78). Instead of terminating Mr X's narration, the narrator's interjections help sustain it by soliciting more information or by encouraging Mr X to explain himself. The narrator is therefore implicated in how Mr X chooses to style his material. His framing of Mr X replicates the ways in which the tale is edited whilst attempting to distance himself from what the other represents.

At this point, however, the attempt to read Mr X's social critique as the story's authorial comment comes unstuck. The narrator's inability to manage Mr X as if he were part of his collection – to classify him as an exotic but unrelated item – reproduces a similar ambiguity in the reader insofar as the reader is shocked by the misanthropy of Mr X's tale but none the less *continues to read*. The multi-layered narrative, otherwise elided when Mr X is taken to be the dominant player, resists a one-sided interpretation by foregrounding the subjectivities of the participants and the ironic, or surplus, effects in terms of how the text is framed.

Recent critics, such as Carol Hamilton and Ted Billy, have turned instead to the connections between collecting, aestheticism, and anarchism. Hamilton and Billy accentuate the similarities between the narrator and Mr X to argue that both figures adopt an aestheticized view of human society with the hope of redeeming that reality: "both are utopian and nostalgic, dreaming of a better world in which value is freed from both use and exchange" (Hamilton 1994: 40). Billy's claim (1997: 110), though, that the story satirizes the late-Victorian aesthetic movement is unpersuasive. The narrator's self-description as "a quiet and peaceable product of civilization" (76) and his delight in "the idea of anarchy ruling among anarchists" because "it could not possibly make for efficiency" (80) associate him more closely with the cultural conservatism of Matthew Arnold than with the views of Walter Pater. His valorization of cultural appreciation and civilized behaviour corresponds ostensibly with Arnold's defence of art in *Culture and Anarchy* (1869) against the philistinism of both trade and the uneducated. The narrator's terror at the close similarities between himself and Mr X calls into question his own need for order and hierarchy. Or rather (as described below), the narrator's self-professed allegiance to a notion of civilization is founded upon a purely aesthetic appreciation for the appearance, as opposed to the moral substance (essential in Arnold's conception of art), of a cultured lifestyle.

This type of reading none the less still tends to favour Mr X's position over the narrator's insofar as the narrator's reification of art is shown to be implicated in Mr X's equally disaffected view of human reality: the ironic (and deathly) uses to which cans of Stone's Dried Soup are put or the way in which Mr X savours his *bombe glacée*. It is possible to read the story's deconstruction of the opposition between culture and anarchy as siding with Mr X, for example, when Hamilton writes of the Lady Amateur: "But perhaps she is also an amateur, in Conrad's view as well as Mr X's, because she is a woman" (1994: 38). The attempt to explain away the text's anarchistic treatment of short story conventions as confirmation of Mr X's worldview over the narrator's *bourgeois* orderliness deliberately elides those deviations from the "well-made" story (the text's asymmetrical design, refusal of closure, and tendency towards excess rather than clarity) that make such a resolution impossible. As such, this reading also obscures the story's critique of a pseudo-moral aestheticism, which the narrator espouses, and from which Mr X cannot be divorced.

Daphna Erdinast-Vulcan's recent reading of the story attempts to negotiate Mr X's role within the text by seeing him as "a failed author (an author *manqué*) in that he has turned the real – the suffering, the action, the revolt of his fellow-men – into an aesthetic product for the consumption of his declared enemies" (1999: 123). Mr X openly admits that his fortune has come "not from the millions of pamphlets distributed gratis to the hungry and the oppressed, but from the hundreds of thousands of copies sold to the well-fed bourgeois" (77-78). In that sense, Mr X is a conductor within the circuit of commercial exchange that he otherwise claims to want to overthrow. For Erdinast-Vulcan, Mr X is "the real informer" since he acknowledges his complicity with the capitalist order and even "enjoys the neutralization of his social critique as it turns into an object of art" (1999: 126): the story that he prepares for the delectation of the narrator.

In this reading, Mr X becomes a representative of the *avant-garde* artist insofar as he delights in surfaces (including that of his own authorial role) as he assaults the surface reality of commerce. None the less, his fashionableness as a writer is in the past – "my writings *were* at one time the rage" (78) – so that there is the suggestion that the yarn he spins is designed to disprove or conceal his fading claim to be a writer and a celebrity. In that sense, far from being an informer about the condition of the *avant-garde*, Mr X is vainly shoring up his own authenticity through the medium of his own self-aggrandizing narration. Crucially, for the kind of insight that Erdinast-Vulcan suggests for Mr X, he lacks any ability to empathize with the Lady Amateur's love for Sevrin. Lost within his own rhetoric as "the greatest destructive publicist that ever lived" (74), Mr X exhibits all the characteristics of the sociopath; as expressed in his "rasping, cold and monotonous" voice (76). By contrast, a failed author (at least in financial terms) such as Conrad realizes the impossibility of being an "enemy" in an omnipresent marketplace.

Despite their increasing sensitivity to the text, all of these critical accounts focus on Mr X's deception of the narrator as a critique of, or critical engagement with, *bourgeois* attitudes and economics. With or without eliding the roles of Mr X as the internal narrator and Conrad as the text's author, they tend to favour Mr X's viewpoint as the authorial position at the expense of the anonymous first-person narrator. His role tends to be seen as no more than a conduit for Mr X's views and as a willing dupe. The role of the Parisian friend in, first, fashioning the encounter between the narrator and Mr X and, then, in placing the booby trap (the enigmatic joke) that has engendered so much critical debate also tends to be underestimated. In the most sensitive reading of the tale to date, Keith Carabine has analysed how each of these characters contribute to the system of gestures that, in Conrad's words, bear "not on the facts but on the moral satirical idea" of the story (*CL3*: 305). Carabine extensively shows how both the narrator and his fellow-collector are implicated in Mr X's social disaffection by their obsession with collecting itself: they conspicuously lack a moral conscience as to what or why they are engaged in collecting. For instance, the narrator's praise for "the patience" and "the passion" that his friend brings to the exercise of collecting acquaintances implicates the narrator in the process of reification where human objects are things to be measured and stored "away in the galleries of his mind" (73). The fact that, at the story's close, the narrator is more concerned with identifying the location of the joke than with the human drama of Mr X's tale suggests that he has learnt nothing from what has occurred. Consequently, he is unable to counter his friends' admiration for Mr X since, like them, he lacks the capacity for moral, as opposed to aesthetic, distinction.

Importantly, whereas other critics take the Lady Amateur's association with anarchism as a sign of her dilettantism and thus assume Mr X's judgement upon her to be authoritative – "mere gestures of her class" (101) – Carabine emphasizes Mr X's unreliability in understanding the Lady Amateur's actions. Mr X's infiltration of the *bourgeoisie* is, in part, achieved by his adoption of a set of gestures, a means of conducting and presenting himself in public that the narrator studiously enumerates. His appreciation of the Lady Amateur is, again in part, motivated by a purely aesthetic pleasure in performance but also by his identification with a fellow-actor:

> She had acquired all the appropriate gestures of revolutionary convictions – the gestures of pity, of anger, of indignation against the anti-humanitarian vices of the social class to which she belonged herself. All this sat on her striking personality as well as her slightly original costumes. Very slightly original; just enough to mark a protest against the philistinism of the over-fed taskmasters of the poor. Just enough, and no more. (81)

Although this passage can be read for scorn, Mr X's emphases upon the "slightly original" and "just enough" can also be read for their appreciation. To be too much or too derivative would result in an obviously transparent mask. Instead, Mr X appreciates the ways in which the Lady Amateur balances her performance so that it appears to be true. Equally, in the moment of his triumph, Mr X still manages to praise Sevrin's performance: "with something, too, in his face of an actor intent upon the terrible exigencies of his part" (96). When, however, the love interest that earlier critics have derided as part of Conrad's compromise with *Harper's* appears, Mr X is unable to decipher the action:

> He looked attentively into her eyes. It was the attitude of love-making, serious, intense, as if on the brink of the grave. I suppose she felt it necessary to round and complete her assumption of advanced ideas, of revolutionary lawlessness, by making believe to be in love with an anarchist. … [H]er gestures were unapproachable, better than the very thing itself in the blended suggestion of dignity, sweetness, condescension, fascination, surrender, and reserve. She interpreted her conception of what that precise sort of love-making should be with consummate art. (85)

That Mr X has to "suppose" indicates that he is uncertain of what is happening between Sevrin and the Lady Amateur, or what her motivations might be. He is forced to read rather than to know what is occurring whilst, at the same time, claiming that it is the Lady Amateur who is having to interpret and to assume what to do in accordance with her performance as an anarchist. Mr X's interpretation, however, is contextualized by a deterministic understanding of human history in which social relationships are directed, not by the participants, but by impersonal historical forces.

This ideology allows Mr X to distinguish between his carefully selected array of gestures and that of the Lady Amateur's. Whereas Mr X's ability to detect the traitor is meant to illustrate why his class will become ascendant, the Lady Amateur's performance is nothing but a gesture: "That is why their kind is fated to perish" (101). The tale, in fact, proves nothing of the sort since Mr X's understanding of human nature is nothing *but* an ideology. Its limitations are exposed by its inability to deal with such a genuinely irrational emotion as love:

> [Sevrin] had fallen in love with the accomplished and innocent gestures of that girl. An actor in desperate earnest himself, he must have believed in the absolute value of conventional signs. As to the grossness of the trap into which he fell, the explanation must be that two sentiments of such absorbing magnitude cannot exist simultaneously in one heart. The danger of that other and unconscious comedian robbed him of his vision, of his perspicacity, of his judgment. (93)

At least two important issues stem from this passage. The first is Mr X's objectification of the sentimental as irrational and corrosive. The second relates to a point also raised by Carabine. In describing Sevrin as "an actor" who "must have believed in the absolute value of conventional signs" for the truthfulness of his performance, Mr X positions himself as someone who sees through all signs as "mere gestures." Sevrin's fatal love for the Lady Amateur presents Mr X the opportunity of seeing through Sevrin's disguise. Yet, when Sevrin gives himself away, Mr X is forced to admit of the Lady Amateur "that after advancing a few steps she extended her hand towards the motionless Sevrin. And that at least was no gesture. It was a natural movement" (92). Mr X's contradiction of himself – his tacit acknowledgement that not all gestures are a matter of artifice – emphasizes both his inability to rationalize the naturalness of that movement and the distance between Conrad's authorial position and that of Mr X's.

To return to the issue of sentiment. Mr X's condescending attitude towards romantic love is ironically paralleled by earlier descriptions of "The Informer" as a concession to the mainstream tastes of *Harper's* audience. The twin notions of romance and sentiment are presented as culturally inferior to the rigour and discipline with which Conrad is usually (and approvingly) associated as a key figure in the development of literary Modernism. I would argue, though, that Conrad not only critiques Mr X and his fellow narrators for their lack of moral compassion but also for their lack of sentiment, a sentimentality that is not anodyne but is essential to what Jacques Derrida has termed the "politics of friendship." To do this, I need briefly to consider the role of sentimental fiction and the degree to which "The Informer" both follows and resists the contents of *Harper's*: in some sense, "The Informer" *is* a "pot-boiler" since it uses elements of popular fiction whilst also, in the story's design, denying the mass production of that culture. Returning "The Informer" to its original publication context, as opposed to its later framing as part of *A Set of Six* (1908), highlights the potential dissidence often overlooked in the story.

Although it was Pinker who sold both "An Anarchist" and "The Informer" to *Harper's*, Conrad would have been familiar with the market for which the stories were prospectively written. *Harper's'* mixture of short fiction, serialized novels, and well-written but undemanding articles established it not only as the leading American title of its type but also as a model for its British equivalents such as the *Pall Mall Gazette* and *Strand Magazine*. The kind of story-writing that tends to dominate *Harper's* – sketchy, anecdotal, melodramatic – was representative of much magazine fiction published on both sides of the Atlantic. Reading "The Informer" in its original context (it is bracketed by articles on rural Spain and the "Bloody Assizes") emphasizes just how strange the story is in relation to its contemporaries. Although the final exchange between the two collectors suggests a "twist in the tale," in the style of O. Henry or of Guy de Maupassant's "The Necklace," the reader's inability to place the joke indicates that this is another Conradian parody of short-story conventions. "The Informer" is, in that sense, a conundrum rather than a trick or hoax, as are some of Poe's stories, the conundrum being, perhaps, a more recent development to be found in the work of Kipling and James.

The question, then, is not to what extent Conrad compromised his art to appear in print but how his fiction was ever published. The answer is that though including Conrad would not (in itself) have brought *Harper's* financial rewards, his name would have ensured additional kudos: his work was a valuable commodity in a competitive marketplace. Conversely, although Conrad did not write "The Informer" with *Harper's* specifically in mind, he would have known the kinds of writing preferred by magazines of this type, including a policy of self-censorship. For example, James's accessible novel, *Washington Square* (1880), was his only work to appear in *Harper's*. In that sense, Conrad delivered a story that *Harper's'* editors would appreciate just as Mr X offers the narrator (who knows nothing about anarchism) a tale he wants to hear, "the course of legends and fairy-tales" (77).

The self-consciousness Conrad brought to the writing of the story and his awareness of its place of publication allowed him to diverge from the limited range of emotions that make up conventional romance fiction's stock-in-trade. Critics such as Suzanne Clark have made great play upon the all-too-familiar emphases in Modernist rhetoric upon hardness, austerity, and angularity to argue that Modernism positioned itself against the soft, the excessive, and the fluid in popular culture and in women's writing in particular: "The sentimental is at issue because no discourse can escape appealing to the emotions of its audience, and yet modernist criticism pretended to do so" (1991: 6).[2]

Such judgements are necessarily retrospective and fail to take into account the extent to which Modernist rhetoric was in process during the early years of the twentieth century without any sense of what its final configuration would be. In that sense, the work of early Modernists such as Conrad is implicitly experimental and his engagement with popular culture of particular interest in an (allegedly) post-modern age. Far from positioning himself against the idea of sentiment, Conrad critiques his aesthetes' reification of desire that results, finally, in objectifying the human as is explicit in Mr X's intolerant brand of anarchism. In particular, whereas Mr X characterizes Sevrin's sentimental feelings for the Lady Amateur as the cause of his downfall, Conrad depicts it as the heroic flaw that distinguishes Sevrin's humanity from the heartlessness of a disaffected aestheticism. At the same time, the sentiment that Conrad proposes, embodied in Sevrin's self-sacrifice, far outweighs the vague "sentiment of womanhood" (90) that the narrator espouses.

Instead, the notion of sentiment implied by Conrad approximates Derrida's recent concept of *aimance* that David Ayers has summarized as "a form of loving which goes beyond the socially determined forms of love and friendship, and beyond the existing cultures and traditions of love" (1999: 220). The resolution of a typical romance narrative, in which hero and heroine are united in a symbolic embrace before their eventual union in marriage, defuses the transgressiveness of *aimance* by reintroducing the cultural determination of heterosexual desire and its consummation within matrimony's legal and religious framework. By contrast, Sevrin's self-sacrifice, his willing denial of the possibility of romantic salvation, and his recognition of the impossibility of his desire

---

[2] In her work on Modernist poetry, Potter has shown how the artistic criteria by which Modernism is commonly understood evolved during a period of political and cultural change. See, for example, Potter 2000.

for the Lady Amateur, communicates a deeper, more profound notion of love than that expressed in the conventional closure of romance narrative. Sevrin's *aimance* for the Lady Amateur is transgressive because it resists the cultural determination implicit in the linearity and end-direction of romance: the lover's reward in the returned embrace of the loved one. Instead, by refusing the compensation of romance, Sevrin's love for the Lady Amateur is suspended; it is unconsummated and unmanaged within either the story's cultural or textual frameworks.

This resistance to temporal progression is explicit to the notion of love that underpins Derrida's ethical and political understanding of friendship: "The truth of friendship, if there is one, is found there, in darkness, and with it the truth of the political" (1997: 16). In the *Politics of Friendship*, Derrida begins with a consideration of a phrase Montaigne attributed to Aristotle: "*O mes amis, il n'y a nul ami*." In meditating on this quotation, Derrida concludes that, in Thomas Docherty's words, "*L'amitié* is, above all and in the first place, a matter for the lover and not for the loved" (1999: 64). As Derrida writes: "The argument seems, in fact, simple: it is possible to be loved (passive voice) *without knowing it*, but it is impossible to love (active voice) *without knowing it* ... The friend is the person who loves before being the person who is loved" (1997: 9). There is, therefore, a temporal discrepancy between the two participants: the lover loves "*in advance* of the loved: friendship is an affair of the lover *before* it is an affair of the loved" (Docherty 1999: 64-65). This breach underlines the social sphere: "One can love being loved, but loving will always be more, better and something other than being loved" (Derrida 1997: 11).

Sevrin's relationship to the Lady Amateur can be compared to the lover who loves before the loved one. The existence of this relationship, in which loving is predicated over knowledge, would deny the connoisseurship of the frame-narrators in which knowledge, the weighing and penetration of objects (human or otherwise), is placed above all else. In that context, the Lady Amateur's involuntary response is an *event* in the sense popularized by Jean-François Lyotard, "insofar as it refuses to be absorbed into the *order* of a classical narrative, brought to book in a narrative *account*, its tension exchanged for other tensions" (Bennington 1988: 109). The Lady Amateur's "entreating hand" (93) resists absorption into the ruling narrative framework of Mr X in which all gestures are mere artifice. The very naturalness of that movement is unrepresentable insofar as its meaning exceeds the comprehension of Mr X's limited, over-determined understanding of human nature. As an event, the Lady Amateur's gesture temporarily suspends the forward motion of Mr X's narration. It exists not only as a lacuna embedded within the multiple framing of the story but also as a deterrent to formal narrative progression, the end-direction with which the short story is often associated. As such, the gesture foregrounds the degree to which Mr X, despite his alleged hostility to the dominant social and economic order, complies with a hegemonic emphasis upon progress that finds its analogy in the act of classification pursued by the frame-narrator and his Parisian friend. Conrad's use of an impossibly unrequited love contests more effectively the insistence of *chronos* than any anarchistic attempt to blow up the Greenwich Observatory, because of its deep human drama, the complexity of which is magnified by the extent to which the frame-narrators fail to understand its significance.

As Carabine emphasizes: "buried in X's tale of the gross 'trap' … is another tale … of thwarted love and human misery, that reveals the imbecility of his ideas and the baseness of his judgements" (1999, 38). Sevrin's love for the Lady Amateur is threatened by his inability to dissuade her of the charms of anarchism. As she says, "If I ever felt sure of anything, it was of Sevrin's high-minded motives" (99), her sense of principle being part of her appeal for Sevrin. None the less, swayed by his attentions, the Lady Amateur unwittingly reveals her affections for him and thereby gives Sevrin away. Since Sevrin is unable to declare his love for the Lady Amateur without undermining her faith in him (his appearance of being committed to the cause), he sacrifices himself. As Mr X half-comprehendingly states, Sevrin abandons "his future usefulness" (93), but it is not just his financial reward as an informer that he declines. That Sevrin loses his life is also immaterial; crucially, he abandons any hope that the Lady Amateur will return his love. Mr X's cutting line that Sevrin "was not enough of an optimist" (101) completely misses the point and condemns him for good and all. Lost in the irrational belief that the future is there for the taking, and for the remaking, through the imposition of a minority will over the majority, Mr X is hopelessly committed to an abstract and inhuman notion of historical progress. By contrast, Sevrin's pessimism is a realistic assessment of his chances, which, in its denial of either escape or redemption, articulates a commitment to humanity (to affectiveness) that is otherwise silenced through the frame-narrative. In that sense, "The Informer" accords with its future sub-title of being an "ironic" tale, since Sevrin's vestigial humanity surpasses its suppression by Mr X whilst also countering the frame-narrators' incomprehension and disaffection.

Furthermore, since the love that Sevrin experiences for the Lady Amateur is conditioned by its temporality and thereby its mutability, Sevrin's *aimance* opposes the immutability of knowledge that the frame-narrators valorize at the expense of social intercourse (the narrator's obsession, at the end, with a joke rather than with the human drama). As Derrida argues: "one must first know how to love, and know what loving means by loving" (1997: 11). Precisely this knowledge, an ethical understanding that exceeds rational calculation, is what the frame-narrators so drastically lack and upon whom Conrad's joke (the moral satire of the story) is played. In that sense, without eliding Conrad's political and intellectual antagonisms towards anarchism, "The Informer" can be said to be a genuinely anarchistic text. In a world, as offered to the reader by the frame-narrators, in which reality is objectified as a commodity to be measured and penetrated, Sevrin's impossible love for the Lady Amateur is a truly anarchistic gesture by not only being instinctual, as opposed to artificial, but by also denying its use-value: its consummation in terms of romantic discourse. Sevrin's love is sentimental, not because it is anodyne but because its depth of emotion is complex; it gestures towards an order of love that exceeds the limited knowledges of both romantic narrative and the frame-narrators' understanding of human society. As opposed to the artistic and political dystopias of Mr X and his fellow interlocutors, Sevrin's love is genuinely utopian since it prefigures an order to come but not yet present. His silencing (both physically and textually) bears witness to the strength of his future desire. Equally, the Lady Amateur's gesture is anarchistic not only by being natural in this otherwise commodified environment, but also by resisting its role within the production of Mr X's narrative. In that sense, Sevrin and the Lady Amateur resist more effectively the commercial emphasis upon productivity than their anarchistic and aesthetic counterparts, whilst also embodying values such as love and self-sacrifice that are marginalized within the demand for cultural and economic rationalization. Mr X's dismissal of the Lady Amateur – "she went into retreat in a convent" (101) – is another misjudgement that undermines his over-calculated view of humanity. Her withdrawal, seemingly the clichéd response to guilt and lost love, may instead be the realization in "loving the deceased that the decision in favour of a certain lovence [*sic*] comes into being" (Derrida 1997: 10). Couched in stereotypical terms, the depth of the sentiment loses Mr X, who is now, once and for all, blinded to anything other than mere gestures. Unlike his anarchist-aesthetes, and anticipating Derrida's post-modern ethics, Conrad acknowledges that the significance of social relationship – of love and friendship – is that it is founded upon "the brink of the grave" (85).

Acknowledgements

I should like to thank Maggie Awadalla, Jennifer Ballantine-Perera, and Keith Carabine for helpful comments on a draft of this essay, and Rachel Potter for bringing Suzanne Clark's work to my attention.

Works cited

Ayers, David. *English Literature of the 1920s*. Edinburgh: Edinburgh University Press, 1999.

Bennington, Geoffrey. *Lyotard: Writing the Event*. Manchester: Manchester University Press, 1988.

Billy, Ted. *A Wilderness of Words: Closure and Disclosure in Conrad's Short Fiction*. Lubbock: Texas Tech University Press, 1997.

Carabine, Keith. "'Gestures' and 'The Moral Satirical Idea' in Conrad's 'The Informer.'" *Conradiana* 31.1 (1999): 26-41.

Clark, Suzanne. *Sentimental Modernism: Women Writers and the Revolution of the Word*. Bloomington: Indiana University Press, 1991.

Derrida, Jacques. *Politics of Friendship*, translated by George Collins. London: Verso, 1997.

Docherty, Thomas. *Criticism and Modernity: Aesthetics, Literature, and Nations in Europe and Its Academies*. Oxford: Oxford University Press, 1999.

Erdinast-Vulcan, Daphna. *The Strange Short Fiction of Joseph Conrad: Writing, Culture, and Subjectivity*. Oxford: Oxford University Press, 1999.

Gibson, Andrew. "Ethics and Unrepresentability in 'Heart of Darkness.'" In *Conrad and Theory*, edited by Andrew Gibson and Robert Hampson. Amsterdam – Atlanta: Editions Rodopi, 1998.

Graver, Lawrence. *Conrad's Short Fiction*. Berkeley: University of California Press, 1969.

Hamilton, Carol Vanderveer. "Revolution from Within: Conrad's Natural Anarchists." *The Conradian* 18.2 (1994): 31-48.

Hepburn, Allan. "Collectors in Conrad's 'The Informer.'" *Studies in Short Fiction* 29 (1992): 103-12.

Potter, Rachel. "Waiting at the Entrance to the Law: Modernism, Gender, and Democracy." *Textual Practice* 14.2 (2000): 253-63.

Scanlan, Margaret. "Language and Terrorism in Conrad's 'The Informer.'" *Conradiana* 27.2 (1995): 115-22.

Walton, James H. "Mr X's 'Little Joke': The Design of Conrad's 'The Informer.'" *Studies in Short Fiction* 4 (1967): 322-23.

Rehabilitating "The Brute"

Michael Lucas
Universidad del Bio-Bio, Chile

CONRAD COMPLETED "The Brute" in January 1906. It first appeared that year in the *Daily Chronicle*, was reprinted in 1907 in the United States in *McClure's Magazine*, and was then collected in *A Set of Six*, published in 1908.

Never, to my knowledge, has a good story been more often dismissed or ignored in critical writing. Baines considers it "a slight story, little more than a pot-boiler" (1960: 388). Graver's opinion is that it is "the least substantial" piece in *A Set of Six* (1969: 132). Fleishman (1967) judges it to have little literary or political interest. Watts, who dismisses it thus: "then Conrad offered [to Blackwood] one of his worst tales, 'The Brute', which was properly rejected" (1989: 77), later adds: "The 'degrading' of his creativity can be seen not only in trivial fiction for the market (tales like 'The Inn of the Two Witches,' 'The Brute' or "Gaspar Ruiz)" (131). Gail Fraser dismisses the story, along with "Gaspar Ruiz," "An Anarchist," and "The Informer" as "essentially anecdotal" (1996). And Batchelor condemns the story as "a pot-boiler about a dangerous ship, written for the (substantial) audience which liked Conrad's Old Salt narratives" (1994: 150). None of these critics produce evidence for their evaluations, and one is tempted to dismiss these comments as casual personal opinions.

The purpose of this essay is to show that Conrad's own dismissal of the story, which seems to have been taken too seriously by the critics, should be taken with a pinch of salt. After all, some of his comments about the volume *A Set of Six*, as well as about some of his other works, are uninformative, dismissive, misleading, or even absurd. For instance, he wrote to Wells about *A Set of Six*: "I've been writing silly short stories" (*CL3*: 297) and to Sir Algernon Methuen: "They are not studies – they touch no problems. They are just stories in which I've tried to be *simply entertaining*.... All but two draw their significance from the love interest" (*CL4*: 29-30).

I think it is interesting for us, to consider this story, as Cuthbertson (1974) does, in the context of the other five stories in *A Set of Six*. This volume has often been criticized for being not so much a "set" as a rag-bag: that the six stories, apart from the same author, share no feature or common ingredient.

The first in the volume, "Gaspar Ruiz," set in Chile at the time of *la guerra a muerte* in the second decade of the nineteenth century, has the length of a longish short story but, divided into twelve chapters, has the structure of a novel. Its narrative mode vacillates between first-person narration by a Chilean general and anonymous third-person omniscient narration. Critics universally agree that this is a poor work. It appears to be a rough sketch for a full-length piece of popular exotic romance fiction such as Rider Haggard's *Montezuma's Daughter* or *She* or the Ford-Conrad collaboration *Romance*. The second story, "The Informer," set in London, has engendered considerable critical disagreement. Much more interesting than "Gaspar Ruiz" in several respects, it has attracted serious criticism.[1] It has a typically Conradian narrative structure, with a written narrative framing a simulated oral main narrative. The narrator of the former portrays the narrator of the latter, Mr. X, as an unscrupulous hypocrite whose reliability as a narrator is explicitly questioned at the very end of the story. The story also has its share of Conradian irony, as in *The Secret Agent*, specifically at the expense of anarchists. "The Brute," the third story, is followed by "An Anarchist," whose complex narrative structure shows how skillfully Conrad bestowed individual voices on his characters in his short fiction. The fifth, the rather longer story "The Duel," set in the Napoleonic and post-Napoleonic France, concerns an absurd and protracted quarrel between two officers of the *grande armée*. The story is told by a third-person omniscient narrator throughout. The last in the "set," "Il Conde," features a first-person narrator who tells of his meeting with an old aristocrat from Central Europe who, on a visit to Naples, is threatened by a young man with a knife. This incident and its consequences are ambiguously reported by the narrator on behalf of the protagonist.

"The Brute," then, finds itself in very mixed company, and attempts to link the stories thematically have not been entirely convincing

---

[1] See, for example, Scanlan 1995 and Carabine 1999.

or at such a level of generality that they tell us little. One such attempt is Cuthbertson's (1974), which sees three rather tenuously unifying themes: freedom, absurdity, and destruction. He says of "The Brute" that it "can be viewed best as political theory and as an example of the absurd terror .... *The Brute* is an absurd ship, a murdering ship" (51). He goes on:

> "The Brute" is one of Conrad's few stories to focus on an object rather than a person. It would be significant for that cause alone. There is more than a venial bit of "pathetic fallacy," for *The Apse Family* is struggling for freedom from its owners. Freedom, most especially on the part of an inanimate object, is lunacy. ... Given the political context of Conrad's thought, the conclusion is mandatory. The ship must destroy itself on the rocks. (51)

I am not sure who or what Cuthbertson intends us to understand is the exhibitor of this lunacy. The ship? The narrator? Conrad himself? Or the reader who swallows the notion of a ship struggling for freedom?

All the story's critics appear to have overlooked its demonstration of Conrad's masterly narrative technique. The critic who most recognises this is Carabine:

> All his [Conrad's] short stories ... even when packed full of "incident," such as ["The Informer"] and "An Anarchist" in *A Set of Six*, are "studies" because their double narratives foreground the problematics of interpretation for both narrators and readers. (1999: 26)

The implication is that "The Brute," as one of the stories with a double narrative, has value because it is such a study.

The story is quite complex both in its plot and narrative structure, which are closely bound together. There are three plots: the frame plot, the vehicle for the other two, which may be called the "Maggie plot" and the "Wilmot plot." The frame plot is narrated by an anonymous narrator who enters the inn The "Three Crows" on a rainy day, presumably around lunchtime. He then joins three men in the parlour and listens to the narrative, already started, of one of them, a "stranger in tweeds" (106), later identified as Ned, a new customer of the inn.

The two plots of Ned's simulated oral narrative are linked sequentially, the first leading into the second. The "Maggie plot" includes the early history of a ship, *The Apse Family*, which, because of its unpredictable movements, causes a death on every voyage, culminating with that of Maggie Colchester, the niece of the captain and the betrothed of Charley, Ned's elder brother. The "Wilmot plot" is something of a coda about how *The Apse Family* finally met its (or her) end. An important difference between the narration of these two plots is that the first is narrated largely from first-hand knowledge, whereas the second is based on the narration by Wilmot, the officer whose negligence and sexual proclivities led to the ship's destruction.

Like "Youth," "Heart of Darkness," "Falk," and "The Informer," amongst others, "The Brute" has a frame-narrator and a main narrator, both autodiegetic. The frame is a clear case of written narration, as the story's opening lines show, with their clause-initial participial phrases:

> Dodging in from the rain-swept street, I exchanged a smile and a glance with Miss Blank in the bar of the Three Crows. This exchange was effected with extreme propriety. It is a shock to think that, if still alive, Miss Blank must be something over sixty now. How time passes!
>
> Noticing my gaze directed inquiringly at the partition of glass and varnished wood, Miss Blank was good enough to say, encouragingly:
>
> "Only Mr. Jermyn and Mr. Stonor in the parlour, with another gentleman I've never seen before." (105)

The main narrator, however, is presented explicitly as an oral narrator, the teller of a tale – purportedly a true one – to an audience of three in an inn. The narration's oral quality is evident in the following example:

> "Eh! Why not? Why couldn't there be something in her build, in her lines, corresponding to – What's madness? Only something just a tiny bit wrong in the make of your brain. Why shouldn't there be a mad ship – I mean mad in a ship-like way..." (112)

The reader has reason to doubt the reliability of both narrators. Is the frame-narrator lacking in perspicacity in allowing himself to be deceived about the reference of the female pronouns in the earlier passages of Ned's narrative that he listens to? Or is Conrad's deception impenetrable, too clever for even the most perspicacious reader or listener? Whom does Conrad deceive? Just the frame-narrator? Or everybody except Stonor and Jermyn, who have heard the beginning of Ned's narrative? Does he deceive Miss Blank, whose stifled yawn in response to a statement of Ned's that shocks the frame-narrator suggests that she also heard the beginning of Ned's narrative?

And what about Ned? Is he trickster or is Conrad? Is Ned a joker like Mr. X in "The Informer"? Does he deliberately withhold from the frame-narrator the identity of "she"? Or is Ned not guilty of deliberate deception – a contrivance of Conrad's to deceive the reader?

That such questions are raised is not evidence that "The Brute" is a sloppily written story like "Gaspar Ruiz." Rather, they occur because of the interest of Conrad's narrative technique and his use of it to test the reader's involvement and comprehension.

There follows an attempt to answer this rash of questions.

I cannot accept that Ned is an unreliable narrator in the sense that he enjoys playing tricks on his narratees. His story is too tragic, and he is too involved in its events for him to deceive the frame-narrator deliberately and for the fun of it. If any narrator is unreliable, it is the frame-narrator, who is deceived – like the reader – by the continual use of unresolved anaphora in the form of the female pronouns "she" and "her." The frame-narrator is deceived, not deliberately by Ned, but by Conrad himself.

Conrad must have been amused when he first discovered that, in a language lacking a complete system of grammatical gender, ships were referred to by female pronouns. He was surely sensitive to this because grammatical gender is an obligatory feature in his first and second languages, Polish and French, occurring systematically in every noun phrase. In both, speakers and writers are forced to choose between masculine and feminine (and, in Polish, also neuter). In English, gender is generally optional, systematically obligatory only in third-person singular pronouns. This curious feature must have seemed to afford the possibility of an amusing trick that could be played on his readers. This trickiness, which we find also in the final lines of "The Informer," as well as in "Il Conde," as Carabine points out (1999) could be looked on as a device to ensure acceptance by editors of popular magazines, but Conrad's use of it is flawless and does not debase the story.

I want to look more closely at the trick that Conrad, through the unwitting Ned, plays on the frame-narrator and the reader. What does the frame narrator imagine is the referent of the female pronouns? The first thing he learns from Ned is that "she" is the victim of a brutal attack by Wilmot, who "fairly dashed her brains out" (105). It seems, though, that "she" deserved it, at least from Ned's point of view, first, because "she did her best to break up [his] pluck," and, secondly, because "she jolly near drove as fine a fellow as ever lived into a madhouse" (107). "She" is a serial killer, or perhaps a terrorist, "going about the world murdering people" (107). "She" is a property owner, possessing three houses, one so conspicuous, being big, ugly, and white, that it can be seen "from miles away – sticking up" (107). "She" has an extremely odd relationship with Captain and Mrs. Colchester. There is a hint, or an implication, that "she" provides Mrs. Colchester and her husband with accommodation in one of her three houses, which are not in England because in England Mrs. Colchester "just made shift to hang out anyhow in some cheap hotel or boarding-house" (108). But more unorthodox than this landlady-tenant relationship is the human relationship: Is "she" Captain Colchester's mistress? He was "not you may call in his first youth," and in his wife's judgement "he wouldn't be able to get hold of another (as he used to say) so easily" (108). From this it seems that Mrs. Colchester not just condones but encourages her husband's extramarital affair.

Even when the frame-narrator demands elucidation, it is not forthcoming, not because Ned is uncooperative but because his reply, "I am talking of the Apse family" (109), is unintentionally ambiguous. (Conrad prolongs the reader's bewilderment by not indicating typographically – with italics or inverted commas – that The Apse Family is the name of a ship.)

A further feature of the narration of "The Brute" is that it is unusually dynamic. So often in Conrad's fiction a work opens with a passage of static description, as in "Youth," *Lord Jim*, *Typhoon*, "Falk," "Amy Foster," "The Secret Sharer" and *Nostromo*, or with the narrator's reflections, as in "An Anarchist," "Gaspar Ruiz," "The Informer," and *Under Western Eyes*. And similar passages are liberally scattered throughout the longer works. But in the case of "The Brute," the dynamism of the narration extends from the very first sentence – "Dodging in from the rain-swept street, I exchanged a smile and a glance with Miss Blank in the bar of the Three Crows" (105) – to the very end of the short story: "On going out I exchanged a glance and a smile (strictly proper) with the respectable Miss Blank, barmaid of the Three Crows" (131). And this dynamism is not interrupted by any extended – or even short – passages of static description or narratorial contemplation. These ingredients are blended into the flow of the dynamic narrative so that the reader is neither distracted from the series of events nor caused to feel a lack of support for an imaginative interpretation or distance from the narrators.

In my essay on "An Anarchist" (1996) I have demonstrated that Conrad's style in that story is very different in several respects from his style in most of the rest of his fiction. Although I have not carried out on "The Brute" the detailed linguistic analysis that I used in my study of "An Anarchist," my firm impression is that the two stories share the same spare style, with much lower frequencies of occurrence of adjectives, adverbs, and other grammatically optional modifying elements and structures – what I have called "comment modifiers." Yet in the two stories, and in "The Brute" especially, Conrad's prose does not lose its vividness: he still manages to make us "see." "The Brute" contains one of the most vivid and horrifying scenes in the whole of Conrad's fiction – the death of Maggie:

> [The anchor] had been lowered properly into its hardwood beds, but there had been no time to take a turn with it. Anyway, it was quite secure as it was, for going into dock; but I could see directly that the tow-rope would sweep under the fluke in another second. My heart flew up right into my throat, but not before I had time to yell out: "Jump clear of that anchor!"
>
> But I hadn't time to shriek out her name. I don't suppose she heard me at all. The first touch of the hawser against the fluke threw her down; she was up on her feet again as quick as lightning, but she was up on the wrong side. I heard a horrid scraping sound, and then that anchor, tipping over, rose up like something alive; its great, rough iron arm caught Maggie round the waist, seemed to clasp her close with a dreadful hug, and flung itself with her over and down in a terrific clang of iron, followed by heavy ringing blows that shook the ship from stem to stern – because the ring stopper held!
>
> "How horrible!" I exclaimed. (123-24)

This horrifying episode is described through the medium of Ned's simulated oral narrative, and a convincing simulation it is, with its everyday expressions – "my heart flew up to my throat" and "from stem to stern"; its phrasal verbs – "yell out" and "shriek out"; and its noun phrases containing emotive and subjective adjectives – "a horrid scraping sound," "a dreadful hug," and "a terrific clang." All these give an authentic ring to the narration as that of a mariner telling his true tale to fellow mariners in an inn. This colloquial style is maintained throughout Ned's narrative.

In my essay on "An Anarchist," I demonstrate Conrad's skill, at least in his shorter works, in giving individual voices to his characters and even blending them when one narrator relates the narrative of another narrator, and in a paper given at the Joseph Conrad Society (UK) conference in 1999 on dialogue in Conrad, James, and Ford, I presented evidence that Conrad's dialogue is closer to spontaneous real-life dialogue than the dialogue of the other two writers. In other words, Conrad had a very perceptive ear for the spoken word in English discourse so that in his fiction he could simulate it with considerable accuracy.

Literary critics often seem to favour the sophisticated and witty dialogue among sophisticated and witty upper-class characters that we find in the writings of James and Wilde and consequently underrate Conrad's more functional, realistic dialogues and oral narratives such as those coming from the mouths of mariners like Ned and Marlow. Conrad's exposure to spoken English was not as varied and comprehensive as that of native speakers like James or Ford, but he was in full command of the English of mariners that he had listened to and tried to emulate during his years at sea. This is the variety of English Conrad assigns to Ned's narrative in "The Brute." Here, taken at random, is a sample, illustrating Conrad's skill in handling the casual register that a ship's officer (retired) would use in the company of other seafaring men whom he had not met before:

> "Here" was a jeweller's shop. I couldn't imagine what he could want there. It seemed a sort of mad freak. He thrusts under my nose three rings, which looked very tiny on his big, brown palm, growling out –
>
> "For Maggie! Which?"
>
> I got a kind of scare at this. I couldn't make a sound, but I pointed at the one that sparkled white and blue. He put it his waistcoat pocket, paid for it with a lot of sovereigns, and

> bolted out. When we got on board I was quite out of breath. "Shake hands, old chap," I gasped out. He gave me a thump on the back. "Give what orders you like to the boatswain when the hands turn-to," says he; "I am off duty this afternoon." (120)

Thus far the case for re-evaluating "The Brute" has been made on the grounds of its being a manifestation of Conrad's mastery of narrative technique. The question that needs to be tackled is whether this sophisticated technique is wasted on a story of little significant content. Most critics imply this by their dismissal of the story. Edward Said's comment is relevant here: "Conrad's virtuosic skill in narrative management, which reaches its apex in *Chance*, is always as important as – and usually more interesting and important than – any information the tale conveys" (1974: 125). Thus, even if the story's content were deficient, it would be worth reading because of its narrative structure – an idea that echoes Carabine's words cited above.

Let us now turn to the themes of the story to see if it is more than just an example of Conrad's exercising his narrative skill.

"The Brute" is based on two themes, which are often linked in Conrad's fiction, but especially closely in this short story. The first is a favourite Conradian (as well as Shakespearean) theme: anarchy leads to disaster. Manifestations of this theme occur elsewhere in Conrad's fiction, notably in "An Outpost of Progress," "An Anarchist," "The Informer" and, of course, *The Secret Agent.* The second theme is that when women are involved there is a potential for disaster. This theme is found throughout Conrad's works, and with special force in *An Outcast of the Islands*, "The Lagoon," "Karain," "Amy Foster," "Gaspar Ruiz," "The Planter of Malata," *Victory*, and *The Rescue.*

In "The Brute," the potential for anarchy lies in the presence of a woman in a ship. This is hammered home in this story by the fact that there are three cases. The first is that of Mrs. Colchester, a forthright and opinionated woman, who chooses to ignore the malevolent character of *The Apse Family.* It is her influence that prolongs her husband's captaincy of the ship. The second case is that of Maggie. She is no ordinary young woman: she is the niece of Captain and Mrs. Colchester and because of her vivacity and her beautiful blonde hair is very popular with the crew. She is also self-willed and stubborn and has a disregard for authority and the ship's order. Charley, who has just become her *fiancée*, is unable to control her, and, with tragic consequences, she ignores his order to get off the forecastle head. The ship, being an unmanageable and unpredictable female, cannot co-exist with another unmanageable and unpredictable female, and thus Maggie must be eliminated. The third case is that of the green-eyed governess of the Pamphilius children, who distracts Wilmot during the night when he is in command of the ship on her final voyage. Ned, reporting what Wilmot has told him, suspects that Wilmot and the green-eyed girl had a relatively long-standing relationship and that Wilmot got her the job of minding the Pamphilius children so that they could be in the ship together in order to continue their affair.

One might generalize from these three cases that the women are in control: Mrs. Colchester controls her husband by not allowing him to give up the captaincy of *The Apse Family*; Maggie controls her *fiancé*, in ignoring his request to move to another part of the ship; and the green-eyed girl controls Wilmot, distracting him when he was on duty so that the ship goes on the rocks. We might extrapolate to include Miss Blank, who "controls" "The Three Crows," and the ship *The Apse Family*, a "female" (at least linguistically) in control of the lives of all who sail in her.

Two factors seem to have influenced critics' attitudes towards *A Set of Six* in general and "The Brute" in particular. The first, already mentioned, is Conrad's own derogatory comments about the volume, such as "I've been writing silly short stories." The other factor is the demonstrably inferior quality of the volume's first story, "Gaspar Ruiz," a potboiler if ever there was one, and one that for most critics casts a shadow over the other five stories. It is interesting to speculate what critics would have said if Conrad had not expressed any evaluation of the six, and if "Gaspar Ruiz" had been last in the volume or omitted altogether, with "The Informer" or "An Anarchist" appearing first.

Acknowledgement

A version of this paper was delivered at the Twenty-Ninth Annual International Conference of the Joseph Conrad Society (UK), London, July 2003.

Works cited

Baines, Jocelyn. *Joseph Conrad: A Critical Biography*. London: Weidenfeld & Nicolson, 1960; rpt. Penguin, 1971.

Batchelor, John. *The Life of Joseph Conrad*. Oxford: Blackwell, 1994.

Booth, Wayne C. *The Rhetoric of Fiction*. 2nd edn. Chicago: University of Chicago Press, 1983.

Carabine, Keith. "Introduction" to *Joseph Conrad: Selected Short Stories*. vii-xxvii. London: Wordsworth Classics, 1997.

———. "'Gestures' and 'The Moral Satirical Idea' in Conrad's 'The Informer.'" *Conradiana* 31.1 (1999): 26-41.

Cuthbertson, Gilbert M. "Freedom, Absurdity, and Destruction: The Political Theory of Conrad's *A Set of Six*." *Conradiana* 6.1 (1974): 46-52.

Fleishman, Avrom. *Conrad's Politics: Community and Anarchy in the Fiction of Joseph Conrad*. Baltimore: Johns Hopkins Press, 1967.

Fraser, Gail. 'The Short Fiction'. In *The Cambridge Companion to Joseph Conrad*, edited by J. H. Stape. Cambridge: Cambridge University Press, 1996.

Graver, Lawrence. *Conrad's Short Fiction*. Berkeley: University of California Press, 1969.

Lucas, Michael A. "Dialogue in Conrad, James, and Ford." Paper. Joseph Conrad Society (UK), Twenty-Fifth Annual International Conference, Canterbury, July 1999.

———. Review of Yves Hervouet's *The French Face of Joseph Conrad*. *Conradiana* 28.3 (1996): 233-36.

———. "Stylistic Variation in 'An Anarchist.'" *Conradiana* 28.2 (1996): 86-95.

Said, Edward W. "Conrad: The Presentation of Narrative." *Novel* (1974): 116-32.

Scanlan, Margaret. "Language and Terrorism in Conrad's 'The Informer.'" *Conradiana* 27.2 (1995): 115-22.

Watts, Cedric. *Joseph Conrad: A Literary Life*. London: Macmillan, 1989.

Magic Letters and Mental Degradation: Advertising in "An Anarchist" and "The Partner"

Stephen Donovan
Blekinge Institute of Technology, Sweden

CONRAD MADE LITTLE SECRET of his contempt for advertising. "I must strongly protest against the abominable advertisement being put opposite my dedication," he admonished his publisher in January 1896 after finding an "Opinions of the Press" page at the front of *An Outcast of the Islands* (*CL*1: 261). By the time Conrad made his protest the medium's power over literary production could no longer be ignored or denied. Asking his agent to ensure that the publisher of *Typhoon* made "a certain amount of fuss about the story," Conrad confessed: "The public's so used to the guidance of Advertis[e]ment! Why! even I myself feel the spell of such emphasis" (*CL*2: 319). Indeed, it is a nice paradox that disdain for advertising became an integral part of Conrad's public image, itself carefully promoted in later years.

After briefly sketching the history of late-Victorian and Edwardian advertising, this essay offers a reappraisal of "An Anarchist" (1906) and "The Partner" (1911), two relatively neglected magazine stories written during the difficult years preceding the commercial success of *'Twixt Land and Sea* (1912) and *Chance* (1914). It argues that the representation of advertising in these works evinces critical incisiveness and topicality, and that they anticipate Conrad's sophisticated treatment of the similarly topical theme of finance capitalism in *Chance*.[1] Both stories situate advertising at the cutting edge of an emergent capitalist system organized around *speculation* and *consumption* – figurative terms whose literal connotations of seeing and eating provided the inspiration for these two tightly constructed satires. As I seek to show, Conrad's specific choice of a patent medicine and a patent food reflects not just the ubiquity of these

[1] On *Chance*, see Jones 1999, especially pp. 99-160; Villa 2000; and McCracken 1995.

products in contemporary advertisements but also his dim view of advertising's impact on health and nutrition. More than just melodramatic pot-boilers, the stories can be read as attempts to demystify aspects of advertising and commodity manufacture: in "An Anarchist," branding and the new global corporation, and in "The Partner," venture capital speculation and the modern ad-man.

A World of Advertisements

Advertising grew at breakneck speed in Britain between 1890 and 1920, the approximate book-ends of Conrad's writing career, led by a vanguard of manufacturers eager to forge a new kind of relationship, known today as brand loyalty, between consumers and "repeat purchase" commodities.[2] Advertisers were quick to exploit new technologies such as colour half-tone printing and neon signs as well as marketing innovations such as the publicity stunt and mail-order selling. Advertising's tightening grip on the retail economy was mirrored by its high-profile entry into previously restricted arenas, notably the daily press. Manufacturers began flexing their muscles in the mid-1890s just as Conrad's work began appearing in serials, forcing even the staid *Times* to abandon its policies of limiting column size and excluding display advertisements.

By the turn of the century, everything from hats to holidays was being advertised, and late-Victorian advertising posed important legal and ethical questions. Prior to a landmark court ruling in 1892, an advertisement had been deemed to constitute only an invitation to purchase. Similarly fuzzy regulations governed the widespread use of images of celebrities, especially royalty, and of endorsements by putative scientific experts and enthusiastic but mostly fictitious customers. In every respect advertising was a thoroughly unstable medium when Conrad began writing: at one extreme, it was being accused of polluting the urban environment and of deceiving the buying public; at the other, its posters were being collected, the subject of specialist magazines and even international exhibitions.

---

[2] See Nevett 1981; Fraser 1981, especially pp. 134-46; Richards 1990; and Loeb 1994. On the case for "corporate decision makers" rather than over-production as the impetus behind the expansion of late-Victorian advertising, see Church 2000.

In the early 1900s, contemporary commentators, including advertisers themselves, regularly claimed for it the status of "art," "science," and, if somewhat ironically, "literature,"[3] they devoted little or no attention to the complex processes which would today be discussed in terms of commodification or consumer psychology. Although this lacuna can partly be attributed to the more pressing concerns of fraudulent promises and product adulteration, it clearly also involved a lexical and conceptual deficit. The only reference to advertising in J. A. Hobson's pioneering study *The Psychology of Jingoism* (1901), for example, is the observation that "the mechanical rigidity of print" lends newspaper advertisements an undeserved "degree of credit" (10). Perhaps the methods adopted by advertisers were simply too novel to allow easy analysis. Whatever the case, it lends a double significance to the thematizing of advertising in contemporary fiction. More than just visible traces of advertising's influence on literary production, themselves now being marketed as (and, in magazines, alongside) advertised commodities, they constitute some of the first attempts to measure the medium's impact on citizens of the modern world.[4]

"An Anarchist"

"An Anarchist" is the story of a convict named Paul, who escapes from an island prison off the coast of French Guiana during a riot only to find himself a *de facto* prisoner on another island. After rescuing him from being trampled by cattle, Harry Gee, manager of the Marañon estate, cynically spreads a rumour that Paul is an anarchist as a way of forcing the former mechanic to stay on without salary. Unknown to Gee, Paul has, in fact, been associated with anarchists, albeit through bad luck rather than conviction, and a fear of being murdered by his old comrades makes him decline the narrator's offer of passage home. Tormented by

[3] See, for example, Bridgewater 1910; Calkins and Holden 1905; Findlay 1892; and Day 1897. The American trade journal of these years was titled *Art in Advertising* (1890--).

[4] Wicke 1988 suggests that the period 1850 to 1920 can be seen as marked by a "discursive rivalry and mutual interdependence" between literature and advertising, after which the latter emerged as a wholly self-constituted "universe of discourse" (173).

frustration and insomnia, he lives out his days as "the anarchist slave of the Marañon estate" (161).

Published in *Harper's Magazine* in August 1906, the story, Conrad confessed, was written "carelessly in a temper of desperation" (*CL3*: 300). Such feelings possibly prompted appending the subtitle "A Desperate Tale" to the version collected in *A Set of Six* (1908), although it may also recall the French expression *une histoire désespérée*, a hopeless story. Although Norman Sherry has shown that Conrad adapted material from anarchist newspaper reports of a convict uprising on Ile St-Joseph in October 1894 (220-27), no contemporary source has been identified for the cattle estate, which does, however, bear a resemblance to the Brazilian island of Ilha de Marajó in the Amazon delta.[5]

Although favourably reviewed,[6] "An Anarchist" has attracted little critical attention, most critics being likely to echo Sherry's view that its anticipation of the themes of *The Secret Agent* constitutes the main interest of "a strange story, crude and uncomfortable in some of its implications" (1973: 227). Sherry discerns a parallel between "the gullibility of mankind in the face of modern devices of advertisement ... and the gullibility of the working man in the fact of anarchist propaganda" (219). Daphna Erdinast-Vulcan similarly sees a parallel between the anarchist's inability to escape from the plantation and the narrator's own inability to escape from the world of capitalist enterprise the B.O.S. represents. The butterfly-collector's parody of advertising language is, she suggests, "an act of cultural vandalism directed against language itself" (1999: 117). Much, however, remains to be said about the story's political and cultural contexts.

The first of these concerns the firm that employs Harry Gee and indirectly enslaves Paul. In the latter half of the nineteenth century, the real-life counterparts of B.O.S., Ltd played a pivotal role in South America's economic modernization, successfully establishing close client-patron relationships between former colonies and European powers. The abolition of slavery by French Guiana and Venezuela in the 1850s

---

[5] This island of half a million square kilometres lies approximately 500 kilometres from Ile St-Joseph; Paul remembers rowing for two days and sailing for several more. The narrator's description of a neighbouring city "whose name, let us say, is Horta" (137) actively invites speculation as to its real identity. Marañon, the name of one of the Amazon's tributaries, flows through Peru.

[6] See Sherry, ed., 1973: 212, 217, 222.

and Brazil in 1888, for example, was a key stage in this process. As P. J. Cain and A. G. Hopkins conclude, "Britain achieved in Brasil what she failed to bring about in Africa: the conversion of a slave-holding state to one capable of sustaining new and much expanded forms of "legitimate" commerce" (1993: 299). The shadow of this recent history falls briefly on "An Anarchist" in the scene where Paul is rescued from the high seas by a ship crewed entirely by black sailors, what the racist Gee calls "a small schooner full of niggers" (140).

Conrad wrote "An Anarchist" in a climate of growing cynicism about modern business and, in particular, the unchecked might of a new industrial entity: the vertically-integrated corporation, supported by vast capital reserves and exercising direct control over every stage in the production process. His suspicion of millionaires was fuelled by their seeming affinity with anarchists as much as what Jennifer Shaddock identifies as their exploitation of anarchists as bogeymen. As radical republicans who opposed state regulation and insisted on the primacy of the economic sphere, some libertarian capitalists must have sounded remarkably like anarchists to Conrad. To be sure, he had already made the violence and injustice of colonial corporations a central motif in earlier works: in "Heart of Darkness" (1898-99), the reality of indentured labour under the legal fiction of "time contracts" (*Youth* 66); in *The Inheritors* (1901), the unregulated financing of colonial joint-stock companies; in *Typhoon* (1903), the slave-like transport conditions of the Bun Hin Company's "seven-years'-men" (12); and in *Nostromo*, the conspiratorial role of financiers and industrialists in national revolutions. As he famously declared in 1907, "By Jove! If I had the necessary talent I would like to go for the true anarchist – which is the millionaire" (*CL3*: 491). Certainly, he had little affection for the industrialist Carnegie, the diamond dealer Julius Wernher, or the food manufacturer Joseph Lyons.[7] *Pace* Harry Gee's talk of making arrangements "in justice to *my* company" (138; emphasis added), B.O.S. no longer bears the imprint of any individual: the cowboys he works with "had no definite idea of the B.O.S. Co., Ltd., which paid their wages" (137). Instead, anonymous shareholders head an organization whose day-to-day running has devolved onto a managerial class of hard-pressed men like Gee, who candidly explains: "I am bound to do my best for the company. They have

[7] See *CL2*: 436, *CL3*: 470, 489-90, and *CL4*: 275.

enormous expenses. ... One can't be too economical in working the show" (140). Such personal tyranny, Conrad implies, is the iron-bound rationale of modern corporations for whom all moral issues can be settled by profitability, Gee's watchword that "It's good for the company" (140). On the state-within-a-state of the Marañon *estancia*, "an island as big as a small province" (137), capitalists are, like Paul's anarchist "comrades" back in Paris, a law unto themselves.

So far, so anarchist. But it is a crucial detail that this particular capitalist produces meat. To be sure, setting "An Anarchist" on a cattle ranch seems self-explanatory in terms of theme: the dehumanized convict, "corralled" (141) and reduced to a kind of "breed" (143), lives under the shadow of execution like the cattle around him. The moral, too, seems simple: modern companies view men as beasts.[8] Indeed, given the narrator's scorn for the crude allegory of B.O.S.'s advertisements, Conrad rather heavy-handedly drives home his story's allegorical nature. The narrator likens the Marañon estate to "a sort of penal settlement for condemned cattle" and describes the lowing of its herds as "a deep and distressing sound under the open sky, rising like a monstrous protest of prisoners condemned to death" (137). By the time the story was published the dire conditions of the meat industry were internationally notorious, thanks largely to Upton Sinclair's highly publicized investigation of Chicago slaughterhouses. Conrad had a low opinion of *The Jungle* (1906): Sinclair's realistic exposé of the industry belonged to "a damnable category of more or less pretentious emptiness" (*CL4*: 127). Closer to home, a shipment of American meat was impounded at Brighton in June 1906 (*CL3*: 335 n4), which prompted Conrad to note: "my long Anarc[hist] Story . . . is becoming topical. Query: Which is really more criminal? – the Bomb of Madrid or the Meat of Chicago" (*CL3*: 333). The scandals of the North American meat industry likely affected public perceptions of its South American counterparts: 1900-1910 saw a seven-fold increase in the amount of South American meat

---

[8] The *Patna*'s German captain in *Lord Jim* refers to the pilgrims he is transporting to Mecca as "cattle" (15). Lambasting the "psychology of commercial undertakings" that led to the *Titanic*'s having too few lifeboats, Conrad noted: "After all, men and women (unless considered from a purely commercial point of view) are not exactly the cattle of the Western-ocean trade, that used some twenty years ago to be thrown overboard on [sic] an emergency" (*NLL* 242).

imported to Britain as well as public criticism of monopolistic behaviour among North American meat trusts (Fraser 153-54).

B.O.S. Ltd is not merely a beef supplier but "a famous meat-extract manufacturing company" (135), the producer of a processed and patented foodstuff. Early twentieth-century consumers were suspicious of new processes such as concentrating, freezing, and tinning as well as of manufactured patent foods. Conrad was no exception. He lambasted the designers of the *Titanic* as grocers who poison their customers with tinned salmon, noting sardonically that "the tinning of salmon was "progress" as much at least as the building of the *Titanic*" (*Notes on Life and Letters* 246). "The Secret Sharer's" anonymous narrator recounts feeding his stowaway companion "tins of fine preserves" – presumably an ironic quotation of their label – which he defines more precisely as "stewed chicken, pâté de foie gras, asparagus, cooked oysters, sardines . . . all sorts of abominable sham delicacies" (127). And in *The Rescue* the prospect of having to live off preserved food is "distinctly unpleasant" (146). Conrad's point is not subtle: whatever the seductive claims of their manufacturers, these products would only be willingly eaten by someone facing imminent starvation. As the narrator of "An Anarchist" notes, "In various parts of the civilized and uncivilized world I *have had to* swallow B.O.S. with more or less benefit to myself, though without great pleasure" (136; emphasis added). Moreover, poisoning by unhygienic or adulterated foods was a real danger in late-Victorian Britain – the Conrads got food-poisoning when they went out to lunch after becoming engaged in February 1896 (Meyers 1991: 136) – and led to the passing of a series of far-reaching Parliamentary Acts. The theme of consuming rotten and alien foodstuffs recurs in Conrad's writing: rancid hippo meat in "Heart of Darkness"; human flesh in "Falk"; dog in *A Personal Record*; and "foreign preserved milk" (13) in *The Secret Agent*.[9]

Whatever their nutritional merits or hazards, processed and patent foods differ from ordinary foodstuffs in relying on advertising to announce their existence and to direct consumers (rather than retailers) to specific brands. In *Harper's*, for example, "An Anarchist" and "The Partner" kept company with advertisements for patent foods such as Bermaline Bread and Brand's Beef Essence. This core attribute of the

---

[9] For the broader significance of Conrad's preoccupation with eating, see Tanner 1976.

edible manufactured commodity structures Conrad's parallel scepticism towards patent foods and modern business methods. In "The Partner," he depicts two entrepreneurs as graduating naturally from the manufacture of wood pulp and tinned fruit to a promotional scheme for a patent medicine. In *Chance*, he includes among de Barral's advertising-fuelled fiascos "a canning Factory on the banks of the Amazon" (81). And in the preface to Jessie's *Handbook of Cookery for a Small House*, written in January 1907, Conrad humorously contrasted the "conscientious cook" whose "labours make for the honesty . . . of our existence" with "fraudulent medicine men" who keep entire nations "in abject submission" by steeping them in "the gloom of vague fears" or what would today be called scare copy (*Last Essays* 147-48).

Conrad repeatedly foregrounds the new power of advertising in "An Anarchist." The narrator prefaces his tale with the words: "B.O.S. Bos. You have seen the three magic letters on the advertisement pages of magazines and newspapers, in the windows of provision merchants, and on calendars. ... Of course everybody knows the B.O.S. Ltd." (135). Harry Gee explains that his motive throughout has been to help defray his company's "enormous expenses": "Why – our agent in Horta tells me they spend fifty thousand pounds every year in advertising all over the world!" (140). After he repeats this excuse, the narrator comments ironically that for a company spending so much on advertising "the strictest economy was obviously necessary" (144). If this remark expresses Conrad's view, the complaint would appear to be that meat-extract advertising is, somewhat ironically, in poor taste. To be sure, the B.O.S. pamphlets "written in a sickly enthusiastic style and in several languages, giving statistics of slaughter and bloodshed enough to make a Turk turn faint" (135) recall contemporary advertising claims such as the Leibig Company's grisly boast that the 200,000 cattle it butchered annually would dwarf St. Paul's Cathedral. And yet Conrad's critique of commodity culture reaches beyond aesthetics and even politics. Advertising's truly disturbing feature in what the narrator significantly calls the "modern system" is the creeping "mental degradation" (135) that its reifying of the English language entails. No longer the brain, it is now the stomach that processes this kind of language, metaphorically *consuming* it just like the B.O.S. which the latter promotes. "I have had to swallow B.O.S.," the narrator insists, "But I have never swallowed its advertisements" (135). This point is reiterated in "The Informer" where anarchist revolutionaries are shown packing propaganda sheets into old boxes labelled "Stone's Dried Soup," an unappetizing yellow powder "once rather prominently advertised in the dailies, but which never, somehow, gained the favour of the public" (*Set of Six* 82). Whether an ideological or a nutritional sham, each depends upon its rhetoric "catching on" to succeed. Not merely a political demagogue, the anarchist mastermind of "The Informer" is thus also "the greatest destructive publicist that ever lived" (74), just as in "An Anarchist" the socialist lawyer who defends Paul gives a "magnificent" (148) speech that advertises himself but damns his client. Advertising ultimately circulates not products but language distorted and stripped of meaning.

Importantly, B.O.S. is not just any company. As explicitly as libel laws permitted, Conrad directed contemporary readers to recognize the real-life meat-extract manufacturer Bovril.[10] There are plenty of clues. Harry Gee charges the butterfly-collecting narrator two dollars per day, but the reference to his company's "capital £1,500,000, fully paid up" (138) establishes that B.O.S. is a British firm. *Bos*, as several critics have pointed out, is Latin for ox, but it also formed the first element in Bovril's composite name, the second being *vril*, the mysterious "life force" in Bulwer Lytton's science fiction fantasy *The Coming Race* (1871). Conrad chose Bovril because of its unique status as an advertised commodity. Indeed, he could not have found a better exemplar of the "enterprise, ingenuity, impudence, and resource" (135) that his narrator describes as hallmarks of modern advertising. Bovril spent a fortune on a range of promotional stunts that included a display of leaflet-packed fireworks which, copying anarchism's own headline-grabbing tactics, warned: "Look Out For THE BOVRIL BOMBS Are About To Be Discharged!" These marketing ploys reached huge audiences. Jessie Conrad's *Cookery For A Small House* (written 1906) contained a recipe for game soup which includes "a teaspoon of Bovril" (67), the book's only mention of a branded product, almost as if to comply with the company's stern injunction that "No Kitchen Should Be Without Bovril."

B.O.S.'s claim to supply everything short of "everlasting youth" and "the power of raising the dead" (136) closely parodies Bovril's endless citing of medical exhibitions, hospital contracts, doctors'

---

[10] The following paragraphs rely heavily on Hadley 1970.

endorsements, and the importance of calorific "body-building." "Bovril repels Influenza," blared an advertisement on the cover of the *Empire Review* in April 1901, whilst another blithely assured readers that "Bovril prevents 'catching colds.' Ask your Doctor!" In an advertisement in *The Times* of 15 February 1905, Bovril announced its "Complete Political Creed," an enumeration of the policies that made it simultaneously Liberal Unionist, Protectionist, Conservative, Radical, Free Trader, Colonial Preference, and Imperial. Furthermore, Conrad's sardonic allusion to "the love that Limited Company bears to its fellowmen – even as the love of the father and mother for their hungry fledglings" (135) echoes the firm's efforts to cloak itself in an aura of fraternal selflessness. In one of its most famous images, W. H. Caffyn's 1896 colour poster, the Bovril bull contemplates a jar of meat extract above the caption "Alas My Poor Brother!"[11]

The narrator of "An Anarchist" briefly describes a specimen of B.O.S.'s advertising:

> The "art" illustrating that "literature" represents in vivid and shining colours a large and enraged black bull stamping upon a yellow snake writhing in emerald-green grass, with a cobalt-blue sky for a background. It is atrocious and it is an allegory. The snake symbolizes disease, weakness – perhaps mere hunger, which last is the chronic disease of the majority of mankind. (135)

Although Conrad appears to have invented this example, it closely resembles the style of contemporary Bovril advertisements, which made effective use of the new halftone colour printing process. In particular, the notion of "atrocious allegory" (stamping out disease?) recalls Bovril's fixation with heavy puns and symbolic imagery such as the robust black bull silhouetted against a lighter background of field and riverbank that accompanied its "The Goodness of Bovril" advertisements (Fig. 1). The caption, if not quite promising "everlasting youth" or "the power of raising the dead," boldly proclaims Bovril's new slogan of "Liquid Life" – a literalizing of the motifs of bull (Life) and river (Liquid) as well as a tribute to the drink that Conrad's narrator damns with faint praise as "not really unpalatable" (136).

---

[11] "Oh! my poor brother!" (*Mirror of the Sea* 181).

During these years Bovril became what Hadley calls a "national institution" (3), informing the public in 1903 that its name had entered the English language, supposedly synonymous with "concentrated force." Indeed, Conrad's extraordinary advice to Norman Douglas in 1912 attests to Bovril's unseen influence on literary production: "Don't forget that the E[nglish] R[eview] is meant for the most contemptible part of the populace, that which fills the more respectable streets. They have neither minds nor gullets. You must dilute your stuff. I am perfectly serious. It's like too strong Bovril. Nine people out of ten won't get it down and the tenth man will feel qualmish" (*CL*5: 148). For Conrad's contemporaries, this overwhelming media presence had made Bovril inseparable from the general public. No longer just a meat-drink manufacturer, Bovril had, in effect, extracted, concentrated, and sold the British people themselves. Latter-day opponents of the process of creeping commodification know it simply as *branding*. The obvious exponent of this tendency in "An Anarchist" is Harry Gee, literally a cattle brander, whose sense of humour comprises "the wearisome repetition of descriptive phrases applied to people" (138). To him, the narrator is "Desperate butterfly-slayer" (138) and Paul either "Crocodile" ("he lives half in, half out of the creek. Amphibious – see?") (139) or "Escaped Convict" (141). Joanne Shaddock remarks that the word "anarchist" that delivers Paul into the power of the manager functions as maleficent brand name: "The capitalists in the story ... create anarchists through advertising" (1994: 59). In Gee's banal formulation: "I gave him the name because it suited me to label him in that way" (140). Yet this is only half the story. Although branding was then in its infancy – as evinced by Conrad's scattered references to Waterman and Swan pens (*CL*3: 405), Brand's Meat Essence and Valentine's Meat Juice (3: 456), Rowntree Cocoa (*CL*5: 626), Waterbury watches (*CL*3: 357 and *Set of Six* 282), and Yorkshire Relish (*Twixt*) – its presence was beginning to be felt even in rural Kent: "I do not know into what brand of ink Mr. Henry James dips his pen," remarked Conrad drily in "Henry James: An Appreciation" (1905) (*Notes on Life and Letters* 12). It is here that the historical significance of Conrad's model for B.O.S. lies. By dropping the name Johnston's Fluid Beef, Bovril joined the ranks of Tatcho (a hair restorer), Odonto (a dentrifice), and Tablones (indigestion pills) whose depersonalized, wholly advertising-created identities replaced traditional proprietor-endorsed product such as Mrs S. A. Allen's World's Hair

This and the following Image by courtesy of General Research Division, The New York Public Library, Astor, Lenox and Tilden Foundations

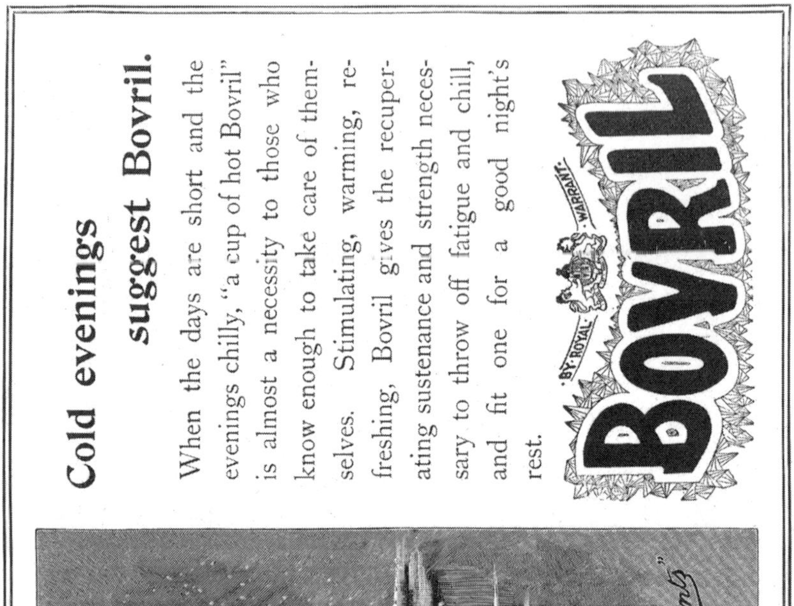
Cold evenings
suggest Bovril.
When the days are short and the
evenings chilly, "a cup of hot Bovril"
is almost a necessity to those who
know enough to take care of them-
selves. Stimulating, warming, re-
freshing, Bovril gives the recuper-
ating sustenance and strength neces-
sary to throw off fatigue and chill,
and fit one for a good night's
rest.
BY ROYAL WARRANT
BOVRIL
BOVRIL
"Defying the Elements"

Restorer, Himrod's Cure for Asthma, and Keating's Powder (all advertisers in *Harper's* August 1906 number).

The holy grail of Bovril branding was the quintessentially British institution of the cup of tea. As the quotation marks in its own advertisement indicate (Fig. 2), Bovril aspired to make "a cup of hot Bovril" the branded equivalent of the national drink that is as much a symbol of friendship and comfort as a form of refreshment. In the words of one "Liquid Life" advertisement: "A cup of Bovril taken after the play, on the golf-links, on the football field, or in any circumstance of deprivation or exposure, not only warms, thrills and stimulates, but ... gives the sustaining, vitalizing power that continues and knows no reaction" (Fig. 2). That even Conrad had been touched by Bovril's grand ambition is clear from the scene in "The Partner" in which the American con-man Cloete seeks to comfort the distraught Mrs Harry Dunbar: ""We are all going together," cries Cloete, all of a sudden. He rushes out, sends the woman *a cup of hot bovril* from the shop across the road, buys a rug for her, thinks of everything ..." (109-10; emphasis added). Cloete's decision to order this hot drink is not merely proof of Bovril's success in marketing its product as the one to reach for in a crisis, it is, like the "three magic letters" of B.O.S. in "An Anarchist" (135) and the "magic word Thrift, Thrift, Thrift" in *Chance* (78), the invoking of brand aura. How appropriate, then, that the only reference to Bovril by name in Conrad's *œuvre* should fall from an ad-man's lips.

"An Anarchist" is much more than a hastily-written melodrama in which Conrad settled scores with a company whose advertisements affronted his aesthetic sensibilities and whose product offended his palate. Rather, it performs an ingenious act of imaginative decommodification, penetrating the advertising sheen of B.O.S.'s noble bull to reveal its brutal exploitation of labour and cynical manipulation of consumers.[12] With its politically subversive message and refusal of narrative closure or easy moralizing, "An Anarchist" signally fails to follow the requirements of fiction magazines, then under pressure from advertisers to publish up-beat tales – what Ellen Garvey calls "fictional worlds as much as possible continuous with the concerns of the ads" (14) – that would put readers in the mood to buy. There is, indeed, a delicious irony in the dismissive term Conrad's contemporaries gave to this process: Bovrilization.

---

[12] Despite Conrad's unflattering portrait of B.O.S., there is no evidence to suggest that Bovril was associated with the meat scandals.

"The Partner"

"The Partner" tells the story of a botched insurance fraud. George Dunbar, a failing entrepreneur, becomes the partner of an American con-man named Cloete, who proposes that they raise capital for a lucrative business project by arranging to wreck a ship owned by George and his brother Harry. When George loses his nerve, Cloete secretly goes ahead with the plan, which ends in disaster: Captain Harry is murdered, and half the insurance money goes to his widow. Inadequately funded, George and Cloete lose most of what remains in the business scheme, only to see investors with deeper pockets take over and make a fortune.

Written in autumn 1910, "The Partner" appeared in *Harper's Magazine* in November 1911. After languishing on the fringe of the Conrad canon, the story has recently been reappraised by readers who discern an intriguing self-reflexivity in both its double narrative structure – a professional magazine-writer relating a story told to him by a stevedore – and the narrator's reference to the necessity of "cooking" such tales "for the consumption of magazine readers" (*Within the Tides* 128). John Batchelor discerns "a surprisingly high level of narrative sophistication and self-consciousness" in the story, which he judges "an interesting and under-regarded narrative experiment" (1994: 221-22). Seconding this view, Robert Hampson argues that its narrative can be read as a complicated parable of writing for serials, "designed to open the reader's eyes to various aspects of the 'business' of magazine-fiction" (1998: 127).

In his 1920 "Author's Note" to *Within The Tides*, Conrad hinted that the story had a basis in "'fact' ... derived from my personal knowledge" (ix), perhaps a reference to the case of Lawrence Wood Cloete whom the *Daily Graphic* reported in February 1891 as found guilty of promoting fraudulent companies (including a South American silver mine). Indeed, Conrad himself had already portrayed unscrupulous financiers in *Nostromo* as well as in *The Inheritors* and "The Nature of a Crime," and he would return to the theme in *Chance*. As his friend Richard Curle recalled, the swindler epitomized "a kind of amoral attitude to life and contempt for humanity which interested him as a novelist" (1928: 159).

And yet the most intriguing aspect of the fraud in "The Partner" is its relation to legitimate business. In directing Stafford, his on-board conspirator, to sabotage the *Sagamore*'s anchor chain, Cloete does more than put lives at risk. He gives himself the edge in a financial contract with Lloyd's which ought to reflect a statistical probability – "They take every risk into consideration" (99), he notes – but which now rests upon a predictive certainty.[13] Marine insurance is essentially a kind of financial speculation, rather like a share option. Possessed of certain facts such as a ship's age and the nature of her cargo, an underwriter guarantees to pay to an owner the insured value of a ship in the event of her not reaching her destination by a certain date. During the voyage, the policy may be sold to other brokers, and if the vessel fails to arrive on schedule the parties may draw up another contract, known as *reinsurance*, based upon the new circumstances. Conrad devotes a whole chapter of *The Mirror of the Sea* to this "market of risks" (61), explaining sardonically how when a ship posted overdue finally arrives, "The reinsurer, the optimist of ill-luck and disaster, slaps his pocket with satisfaction" (62).

In a sense, then, the intended scam of "The Partner" can be seen a bizarre variety of insider trading. For his part, Cloete is quite at ease with the white-collar nature of this crime, and remonstrates with George: "Do I want you to rob the widow and orphan? Why, man! Lloyd's a corporation, it hasn't got a body to starve" (99).[14] In a grotesque inversion of an insurance deal, Cloete negotiates a price for wrecking the *Sagamore* with Stafford – "I don't mean this to have any future – as far as you are concerned. It's a "once for all" transaction. Well, what do you estimate your future at?" (104) – after which the two men seal their arrangement with a drink. Later, the slippery Cloete even tries to default on the terms of this compact by challenging Stafford's claim to have engineered the shipwreck, a quite unnecessary betrayal that he soon realizes to have endangered "the whole business he had set his heart on" (115).

---

[13] Since Cloete expects the *Sagamore* to break from her moorings in Port Elizabeth harbour, Australia, while the crew are safely ashore, it is a nice irony that she runs aground in the English Channel during a storm. There are no sure things in marine insurance, it would seem.

[14] In a letter to Cunninghame Graham of 1922 Conrad describes the recently deceased Lord Northcliffe as having made a fortune without "sweating the worker or robbing the widow and the orphan" (Watts, ed., 1969: 194)

The word *speculation*, derived from the Latin *specěre* (to see), acquired its economic meaning in the late eighteenth century, and its residual connotation of a special kind of seeing has an obvious relevance to maritime business. Speculations, both honest and crooked, are a recurrent motif in Conrad. In "The Partner," it is literalized as a disjunction between how something is represented or advertised, and its true nature. The stevedore begins by explaining contemptuously how tourists "Stare at the silly rocks" (91) while boatmen unwittingly regale them with false accounts of the loss of the *Sagamore* and Captain Harry's "suicide." Upon seeing Stafford's "nasty-handsome" face for the first time, George thinks to himself, "Is that how such a man looks! No, the thing's impossible" (105), as if a less repulsive conspirator would somehow mitigate the crime. When the ship does founder, Captain Harry experiences the curious sensation that "if he were to take his eyes off her she would fall to pieces" (114). Stafford, after shooting Harry and getting into the life-boat, tells the coxswain that the captain has not reappeared on deck because he wants to go down with his ship. The whole drama unfolds, meanwhile, before the transfixed but uncomprehending gaze of Captain Harry's wife, who instructs Cloete, "Tell him I am here – looking on . . ." (112), and whose later derangement originates in the mistaken belief "that her husband should take his own life, with her, as it were, looking on" (123). Again and again, Conrad presents guesses as to the meaning of what is seen, that is, attempts at speculation, as irredeemably wrong. After awkwardly casting about for visual metaphors such as "a Whistler" (92) and "a cinematograph picture" (93), the magazine-writer explains that "I was incautious enough to breathe out another "I see," which gave offence again, and brought on me a rude "No, you don't" – as before" (109).

Conrad identifies advertising with this world of insubstantial speculation in two ways. The first is the nature of the proposed business scheme that Cloete presents as "a patent medicine . . . which with capital, capital to the tune of thousands to be spent with both hands on advertising, could be turned into a great thing – infinitely better paying than a gold-mine" (97).[15] Given the promotion budgets of pharma-

[15] The phrase must have cost Conrad some bitterness to write, having lost his own inheritance of £1,600 in a Johannesburg gold-mine floatation in 1895. On this incident's ramifications, see Donovan, 1999.

ceutical manufacturers at the start of the twentieth century, Cloete's description of a patent medicine demanding "pouring thousands into advertising" (97) seems unremarkable. Nevertheless, the magazine-writer presses the stevedore to disclose the product's name:

> "I am curious," I said, "to learn what the motive force of this tragic affair was – I mean the patent medicine. Do you know?"
>
> He named it, and I whistled respectfully. Nothing less than Parker's Lively Lumbago Pills. Enormous property! You know it; all the world knows it. Every second man, at least, on this globe of ours has tried it. (125-26)

What difference can the brand make to this dismal tale? The fictitious name does evoke the names of real drugs widely advertised in contemporary magazines – Conrad may well have been thinking of Carter's Little Liver Pills – and there is an obvious irony in the idea of marketing "lively" pills with the proceeds of a fatal shipwreck. More importantly, the patent medicine's name supplies a pretext for the narrator to interpellate the reader directly, allowing Conrad to connect the fictional narrative of "The Partner" to the advertisement-dominated world of magazine readers. (He uses the same device in "An Anarchist": "B.O.S. Bos. You have seen the three magic letters . . ." [135].) This is advertising's true "motive force." Not merely can it convince millions of the medicinal value of a quack salve – every other person has *tried* it – but it also creates an illusion of community among an anonymous mass of global consumers.

The second link between advertising and speculation is Cloete himself. Not only has he worked in the patent-medicine trade, he is also a former copywriter whom Conrad takes pains to portray as an advertiser to the very fibre of his being. A careful newspaper reader, Cloete is in his element when buttonholing strangers in the pub in "American fashion" (103) or charming barmaids with his animated expression and "jocular way of speaking" (93), the latter presumably referring to his casual profanity and use of such Americanisms as "cozy" (95) and "funkiest" (102). Crucially, his skill as a raconteur of "little tales" (93) is presented as another facet of his professional vocation. As the stevedore remarks: "Writes advertisements and all that. Tells me funny stories" (94). This copywriter's talent for persuasion, whose similarity to writing fiction has a fascinating resonance, enables Cloete to tempt his cash-strapped partner into crime: "A man who's been in the patent-medicine trade will be up to anything from pitch-and-toss to wilful murder. ... Don't mind what they do – think they can carry off anything and talk themselves out of anything" (94). In an extraordinarily dense metaphor of literal and figurative consumption, the stevedore likens the advertiser's patter to a practised perjurer's testimony: "These patent-medicine chaps don't care what they say or what they do. They think the world's bound to swallow any story they like to tell . . ." (116).[16] As often in Conrad, power is shown to reside in the material force of language. What makes Cloete a killer is precisely what makes him a good ad-man: a limitless capacity to lie, that is, to make people believe – once again, literally "to swallow" – anything. Even so, and notwithstanding the narrator's view of Cloete as "A plausible fellow" (95), Conrad indicates that advertisers could not succeed without the naivety and greed of ordinary people. What Cloete pitches to George as the "Chance of a lifetime" (99) consists only of the doubtful proposition that no one will be hurt if the *Sagamore* is sabotaged, and the ludicrous claim that insurers are less zealous when investigating the loss of ships on which premiums have been paid "for so many, many years" (99). Indeed, his reassurance that the "Wrecking . . . could be managed with perfect safety" (98) sounds like a cheap self-help pamphlet: *Wrecking with Perfect Safety*.

The theme of "The Partner" obviously reflects Conrad's own negative experience of patent medicines. "I am not like Homocea. I don't touch the spot" (*CL2*: 119), he quipped, alluding to the slogan of a popular cure-all. More disturbingly, he related in 1906 how Borys had been "poisoned (through the skin) with the new disinfectant *Lisol* [sic] a most damnable stuff" (*CL3*: 308), and later claimed that the painkiller "CBQ" (Post's Tablets) was making him feel "imbecile" (*CL4*: 187). Patent medicine appears in a correspondingly bad light in his fiction: in *Lord Jim* a patient ignores his doctor's advice in order to indulge in "secret debaucheries of patent medicine" (12); the narrator of "A Smile of Fortune" has an unwelcome feeling that Alfred Jacobus wants to sell him some bottles of "Clarkson's Nerve Tonic" (*Twixt* 40); an offer of

---

[16] On growing demands for the pharmaceutical industry to be regulated, see Fraser 1981: 139-41. On public perceptions over patent medicines as well as the industry's use of advertising, see Richards 1990: 168-204.

two bottles of patent medicine is described by the narrator of *The Shadow-Line* as an "atrocity" (7); and in *The Secret Agent* Mr Vladimir declares ominously that "What we want is to administer a tonic to the Conference in Milan" (27), where an emetic or a poison would be a more accurate metaphor.

Particularly revealing is the way that Cloete's scheme is defined as "the motive force of this tragic affair," since the phrase shifts responsibility for the disaster from an individual to advertising itself, a system that holds out the promise of fantastic profits to the reckless investor, in sharp contrast to the low-risk consols (125) purchased on behalf of Captain Harry's widow. Cloete's American provenance further reinforces the impression that Conrad regarded the real culprit as an influx of new money and alien business practices, epitomized in the stevedore's reference to British ships being sold to "foreigners" (96). (More than one reviewer of "An Anarchist" identified Harry Gee as American, despite the absence of evidence.) Indeed, "The Partner" ought perhaps to be seen as a fable about venture capital investing whereby one business speculation enables another, an appropriate sequel to the theme of "commercial venture" in "A Smile of Fortune" (*Twixt* 85). There may even be an ironic echo of the notion of company "floatation" and product "launches" in Captain Harry's concern that the crew might "attempt to launch one of the ship's boats" (114) and Cloete's fear that George Dunbar's half of the money will "not prove sufficient to launch the medicine well" (125).[17]

"The Partner" is, then, a microcosm of a society in which every human relationship has become distorted, or, more precisely, commodified, by absorption into the cash nexus. Stafford exemplifies this process: a disgraced master mariner reduced to scrounging from a boarding-house landlady, he sells himself to Cloete for £500 over "sixpennyworth of Scotch hot" (104). When he later fails to blackmail his way into doubling this figure, he threatens: "I would shoot you now for tuppence. ... You low Yankee fiend – I'll pay you off some day" (125). In fact, as Cloete realizes, Stafford has already "paid him off" (125) by causing him to lose a fortune "by the price of a revolver-shot"

[17] Just as the *Sagamore* is twice described as having "struck" the rocks (114, 117), Cloete's proposal to George is said to have "struck in his mind" (101). Presumably Conrad meant to write "*stuck*," but the phrase is unaltered in the corrected typescript (The Polish Library, London).

(126). The same pecuniary logic governs Cloete's interaction with the a hotel proprietor where, posing as a considerate ship's agent, he has lodged Stafford at his own expense. His detection of the proprietor's lie about having given Stafford drinks on the house is deeply embarrassing to the publican who, having hoped to advertise his generosity, now risks exposure as a fraud. What matters to Cloete, though, is the realization that Stafford has murdered Captain Harry for his gold. The same principle operates throughout the story: the tourists on the beach buy overdiluted "weak lemonade" (89); the shipping firm of Mundy and Rogers, as the stevedore sneers, "Flew the firm's *house-flag*" (95) as an advertisement on a vessel they no longer own; and the magazine-writer thinks only in terms of what "pays" (92) and deems the stevedore's tale, picked up in a bar, "American fashion" (103), as "not worth many thanks" (128). The only exceptions are Captain Harry and his wife for whom the *Sagamore* has not merely a commercial value but is "our home" (113). The last figures of moral integrity in this sordid world, they are marked out as its victims.

On this view, advertising and the dubious business practices that it encourages are more than just a narrowly commercial evil: they express something fundamental about the changed way in which people relate to each other in the modern world. Advertising has become, in Raymond Williams's phrase, "a true part of the culture of a confused society" (1960; rpt. 1980: 191). Thus Conrad presents the "motive force" of patent medicine advertising as having a necessary corollary in the consumer, personified by George Dunbar's young wife whose "expensive tastes" (97) indirectly cause the catastrophe. Anatomizing her as "silk dress, pretty boots, all feathers and scent," the stevedore describes her house in the suburb of Norwood as "More like the Promenade at the Alhambra than a decent home" (100).[18] That this is refers to a location popular with prostitutes is confirmed by his brutal comment, "that piece of goods ought to have been walking the streets" (100).[19] Tellingly, the

---

[18] On hostility towards suburbia in late-Victorian and Edwardian fiction, see Keating 1989: 320-26, and Flint 1995.

[19] The Alhambra's Promenade was the scene of a "riot" in November 1894 when Winston Churchill and other society "bloods" tore down a screen intended to shield the prostitutes from public view (Stokes 1989). In MS, Conrad portrayed the stevedore as managing two music-halls (Dalgarno 1975).

consumer is just another "piece of goods," a commodity in a commodity-dominated world.

This insight constitutes the real sting in the narrator's oft-quoted closing remark, understandably absent from the serial version, that "This story to be acceptable should have been transposed to somewhere in the South Seas. But it would have been too much trouble to cook it for the consumption of magazine readers" (128).[20] There is, too, a clever *mise-en-abyme* in the idea of retelling a supposedly unprintable story. And yet this is to miss the target of Conrad's thinly-veiled jibe: the fact that where others may simply read, magazine readers must always *consume*. By 1911, *Harper's* and its competitors had long since ceased paying printing and distribution costs with revenue from the cover price but had embraced a system that enabled them to buy "The Partner," a 13,000-word story, for £40, twice as much as Conrad received for the rights to *Almayer's Folly* ten years earlier (*CL4*: 395). Indeed, it is scarcely an exaggeration to say that neither "An Anarchist" nor "The Partner" would ever have seen the light of day without the twenty pages of advertisements – for soap, hair restorers, underwear, coffee, tobacco, baking powder, cocoas, whiskies, disinfectants, toothpastes, and fountain pens – that bracketed the literary contents of *Harper's*. In the process, however, something fundamental had changed. As Conrad understood, short stories in magazines had become advertisements for advertisements.

---

[20] *Harper's* made unauthorized cuts in "The Partner." Dalgarno notes that the final section was added sometime between January 1912 and 1915 "after Conrad had had time to reflect on this history of his text" (1975: 44).

Works Cited

Batchelor, John. *The Life of Joseph Conrad: A Critical Biography*. Oxford: Blackwell, 1994.

Bridgewater, Howard. *Advertising, or The Art of Making Known*. London: Pitman, 1910.

Cain, P. J., and A. G. Hopkins. *British Imperialism: Innovation and Expansion, 1688-1914*. London: Longman, 1993.

Calkins, Ernest, and Ralph Holden. *The Art of Modern Advertising*. London: Appleton, 1905.

Church, Roy. "Advertising Consumer Goods in Nineteenth-Century Britain: Reinterpretations." *Economic History Review* 53.4 (2000): 621-45.

Conrad, Jessie. *A Handbook of Cookery for a Small House*. London: Heinemann, 1923.

Conrad, Joseph. *Letters to R. B. Cunninghame Graham*. Ed. C. T. Watts. Cambridge: Cambridge University Press, 1969.

Curle, Richard. *The Last Twelve Years of Joseph Conrad*. London: Sampson Low, Marston, 1928.

Dalgarno, Emily K. "The Textual History of Conrad's 'The Partner.'" *The Library* (5th series) 30 (1975): 41-44.

Day, Lewis F. "Art in Advertising." *Art Journal* 13 (February 1897): 49-53.

Donovan, Stephen. "Figures, Facts, Theories: Conrad and Chartered Company Imperialism." *The Conradian* 24.2 (Autumn 1999): 31 60.

Erdinast-Vulcan, Daphna. *The Strange Short Fiction of Joseph Conrad*. Oxford: Oxford University Press, 1999.

Findlay, Jessie Patrick. "The Literature of Advertisements." *The Scots Magazine* 9/50 (January 1892): 115-19.

Flint, Kate. Introduction to George and Weedon Grossmith's *The Diary of a Nobody*. Oxford: Oxford University Press, 1995.

Fraser, W. Hamish. *The Coming of the Mass Market, 1850-1915*. Basingstoke: Macmillan, 1981

Garvey, Ellen Gruber. *The Adman in the Parlor: Magazines and the Gendering of Consumer Culture, 1880s to 1910s*. New York: Oxford University Press, 1996.

Hadley, Peter. *The History of Bovril Advertising*. London: Bovril, Ltd, n.d. [1972].

Hampson, Robert. "Storytellers and Storytelling in 'The Partner,' 'The Informer,' 'The Lesson of the Master' and *The Sacred Fount*." *Conrad, James and Other Relations*. Edited by Keith Carabine and Owen Knowles. Boulder: Social Science Monographs, 1998. 123-46.

Hobson, J. A. *The Psychology of Jingoism*. London: Richards, 1901.

Jones, Susan. *Conrad and Women*. Oxford: Clarendon, 1999.

Keating, Peter. *The Haunted Study: A Social History of the English Novel, 1875-1914.* 1989; rpt. London: Fontana, 1991.
Loeb, Lori Anne. *Consuming Angels: Advertising and Victorian Women.* New York: Oxford University Press, 1994.
McCracken, Scott. "Postmodernism, A *Chance* to Reread?" *Cultural Politics at the Fin de Siècle.* Edited by Sally Ledger and Scott McCracken. Cambridge: Cambridge University Press, 1995. 267-89.
Meyers, Jeffrey. *Joseph Conrad: A Biography.* London: John Murray, 1991.
Nevett, T. T. *Advertising in Britain: A History.* London: Heinemann, 1982.
Richards, Thomas. *The Commodity Culture of Victorian England: Advertising and Spectacle, 1851-1914.* Stanford, CA: Stanford University Press, 1990.
Schwarz, Daniel R. "The Lepidopterist's Revenge: Theme and Structure in Conrad's 'An Anarchist.'" *Studies in Short Fiction* 8.2 (Spring 1971): 330-34.
Shaddock, Jennifer. "Hanging a Dog: The Politics of Naming in 'An Anarchist.'" *Conradiana* 26.1 (Spring 1994): 56-69.
Sherry, Norman. *Conrad's Western World.* Cambridge: Cambridge University Press, 1971.
———, ed. *Conrad: The Critical Heritage.* London: Routledge, 1973.
Stokes, John. *In the Nineties.* London: Harvester Wheatsheaf, 1989.
Tanner, Tony. "'Gnawed Bones' and 'Artless Tales' – Eating and Narrative in Conrad." *Joseph Conrad: A Commemoration.* Edited by Norman Sherry. 17-36. London: Macmillan, 1976.
Villa, Luisa. 'Ethos professionale, speculazione e affetti domestici: *Chance* di Joseph Conrad.' *Moderna: Semestrale di teoria e critica della letteratura* (Pisa) 2.1 (2000): 67-98.
Wicke, Jennifer. *Advertising Fictions: Literature, Advertisement, & Social Reading.* New York: Columbia University Press, 1988.
Williams, Raymond. "Advertising: the Magic System." 1960. *Problems in Materialism and Culture.* London: New Left Books, 1980. 170-95.

Territorial Vision and Revision in "Freya of the Seven Isles"

Mark D. Larabee
United States Naval Academy

WHILE GENERALLY DEEMED one of Conrad's less successful works, "Freya of the Seven Isles" boasts a memorable ending. Old Nelson may get the last word, relating the death of his daughter, Freya, from a broken heart; but the image that remains in the reader's mind is that of Freya's intended, Jasper Allen, haunting the beach at Makassar and gazing at the sight of his brig, wrecked on a reef outside the town. Just how that hazard got there deserves investigation, for, contrary to his claims about historical accuracy, this reef did not exist as Conrad portrayed it. Examining previously neglected nautical sources reveals several important topographical manipulations in this work, alterations that Conrad did not acknowledge but that are nevertheless fundamental to the story's artistic integrity.

Setting is far more than a mere backdrop in this tale, whose sources have received scant critical attention. Norman Sherry's influential *Conrad's Eastern World* (1966) and Jerry Allen's *The Sea Years of Joseph Conrad* (1965), otherwise so comprehensive, only briefly mention the story. Later scholars tend to accept without question Conrad's version of the historical setting, or decline to analyze the precise function of the fictional landscape, or both. But evidence indicates that Conrad rearranges certain details of the historical seascape and subjects other aspects to selective description for important symbolic purposes. Conrad's topographical alterations lend this undervalued tale considerably more stylistic subtlety and richness than critics have recognized. Only an awareness, first, of the lengths to which Conrad went to create a carefully organized topography out of manipulated historical facts opens our understanding to the crucial links between the story's physical and psychological landscapes.

Figure 1. The Java Sea.

"Freya of the Seven Isles" is set in the Java Sea, an area Conrad had traversed several times as chief officer in the *Vidar* in late 1887 (see Figure 1). The story's action begins south of Singapore, in the Seven Isles, where Freya Nelson lives with her father. Jasper Allen uses his brig, the *Bonito*, to visit Freya, courting her despite the rival attentions of the jealous Lieutenant Heemskirk, captain of the Dutch patrol boat *Neptun*. After Freya slaps Heemskirk to resist his advances, the Dutchman takes revenge by running the *Bonito* aground within sight of the town of

Makassar on the Celebes. Conrad claimed to have based the ending on an actual incident he had heard about in Singapore, an event that had taken place, he writes elsewhere, no more than five years previously.

Two geographical areas important to the story receive detailed descriptions: the Seven Isles, off the eastern coast of Sumatra, and the waters off Makassar.[1] Some of the topographical features portrayed match the historical reality recorded in pilot guides of the period. In his description of Nelson's home on one of the Seven Isles, for example, Conrad simply adds human inhabitants to deserted islands (see Figure 2).[2] Other than being ringed with reefs, these islands both in their factual and fictive guises are unremarkable. But Conrad repeatedly focuses on these reefs, their spatial relation to the Nelson bungalow, and the curious internal plan of the Nelson house itself, for reasons that I will discuss shortly. At the same time at the other end of the Java Sea, Conrad submits the historical landscape to some remarkable changes.

The approaches to Makassar provide the setting for the dramatic grounding of Jasper's ship, an event that spells the end of his romance with Freya. Off the coast of Borneo, Heemskirk intercepts Jasper and impounds his brig on the pretence of investigating his recent trading with the natives (209-15). The Dutch officer takes the *Bonito* under tow and heads for Makassar. Jasper thinks Heemskirk's "little joke will soon be over" as they head for the harbor: "he is going through Spermonde Passage. We shall be rounding Tamissa reef presently" (218-19). Heemskirk steers for the obstruction and then turns at the last moment while ordering the towrope cut, so that the *Bonito* is carried up onto the

---

[1] This is Conrad's most usual spelling and is followed here. The spelling Makasser occurs in "Freya of the Seven Isles" (209), though this may be a printing error, and Macassar appears in his letter to Garnett. In Conrad's time the name of present-day Ujung Pandang on the Indonesian island of Sulawesi (formerly the Celebes) was variously written as Macassar or Mangkasser.

[2] Findlay's pilot guide (1889) gives this description of the Seven Isles: "Toedjoe, Tudju, or Seven Islands, lie in two groups ... They are high and woody, visible about 25 miles, and surrounded by rocks and reefs. They are uninhabited, but occasionally visited by proas ... Pulo Katjangang, the north-easternmost and largest of the Seven Islands, is 2 miles long ... and less than half a mile broad; it rises to several peaks, the highest of which is 526 ft. above the level of the sea. It is surrounded by a reef, within the limits of which are some rocks above water" (205-06).

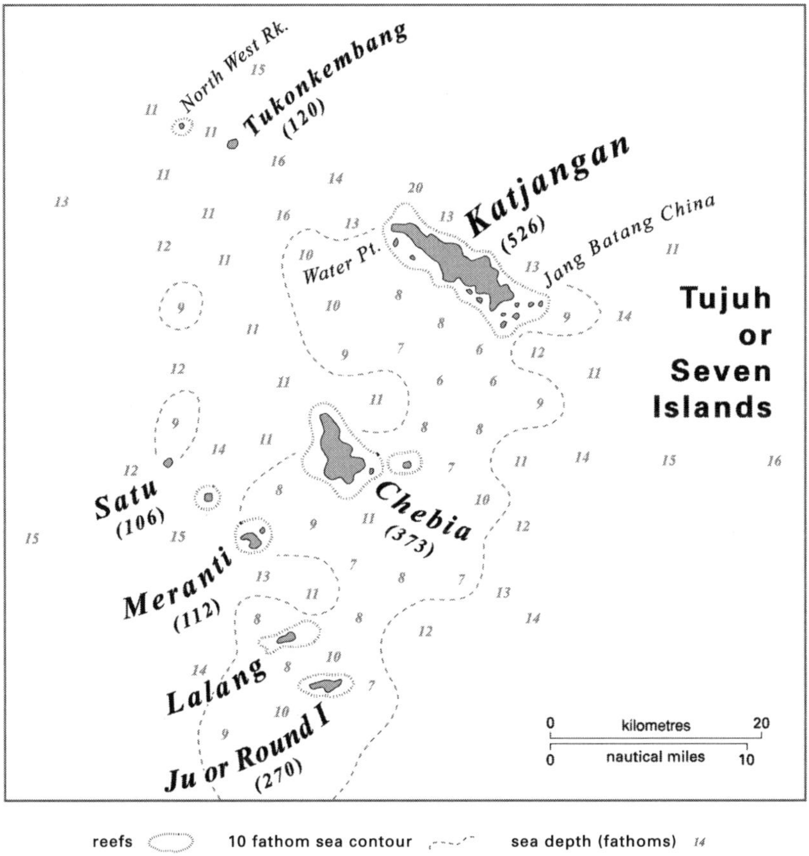

Figure 2. The Seven Isles. Reproduced from British Admiralty, *China Sea: Banka Strait to Singapore (Chart No. 2757)* (London: Hydrographic Office, 1861. Large corrections up to 1897; small corrections up to 1900). Soundings in fathoms.

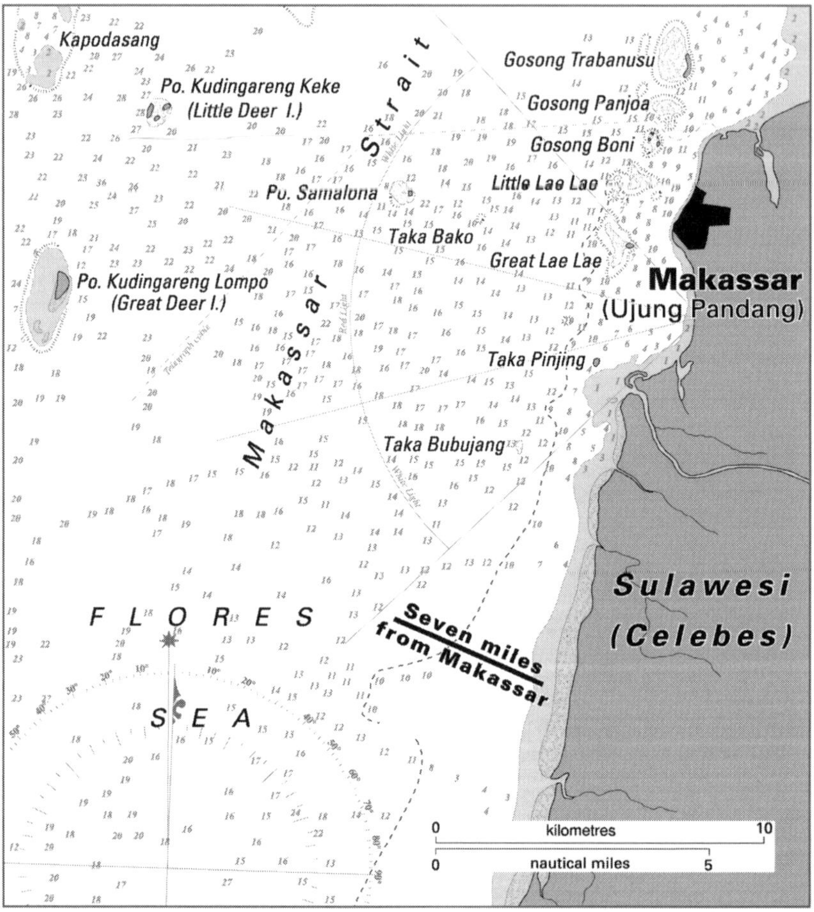

Figure 3. View from Makassar. Reproduced from British Admiralty, *China Sea: Celebes: Approach to Makassar (Chart No. 1293)* (London: Hydrographic Office, 1898. Large corrections up to 1899). Soundings in fathoms; distance in nautical miles.

reef. There she stays, her masts (but not her hull) in clear view of those on shore looking southward. The *Neptun* continues up the passage, anchoring at Makassar thirty minutes later (220).

Conrad makes significant departures from topographical reality in his Spermonde Passage and Tamissa Reef. Spermonde is, in fact, not the name of a single passage, but of an archipelago extending 70 miles along Celebes coast and over 30 miles out to sea. The reefs and islands that make up the archipelago's principal navigational hazards are concentrated north of Makassar's latitude, rather than to the south as Conrad indicates.[3] And there simply was no reef in the described direction at a distance from Makassar that would have given either the *Bonito* or any real-life source a hull-down appearance (see Figure 3).[4] To date, Tamissa

---

[3] Findlay describes the Spermonde Archipelago as follows: "For 70 miles northward of Tanna Keke [an island 20 miles south of Makassar] the shore is lined by a bank extending from 20 to 33 miles off it. Northward of the parallel of Macassar, it is covered with a complete labyrinth of rocks, reefs and shoals, among which are several small islands. It would be impossible to give a satisfactory verbal description of this area, the chart being the best guide" (1889: 782-83).

[4] Figure 3 shows a distinctive feature of the Makassar roadstead: the barrier of coral reefs paralleling the shoreline from Gosong Trabanusu in the north to Great Lae Lae reef just west of the town. The anchorage lay within this line of reefs. Findlay records the two 10-fathom channels, safe for shipping, that pass between the three shoals of Gosong Boni, Little Lae Lae, and Great Lae Lae (1889: 781).

It is tempting to think that this reef barrier, with the narrow channels piercing it, was what Conrad had in mind when he described his "Spermonde Passage" leading past "Tamissa Reef." Today, construction has turned Little and Great Lae Lae shoals into islands; in his picture book of Conrad's Indonesian locales, Braun concludes that this is where the *Bonito* would have been stranded (1970: 21, Photograph 145). But these shoals were much too close to Makassar to give a ship the appearance Conrad describes. It is clear from Conrad's narrative that "Her masts only could be seen"; in other words, the curvature of the earth concealed the hull from view (222). Little and Great Lae Lae were only about a mile off shore, and an observer with a total height of eye of six feet (assuming, conservatively, a person five feet tall standing one foot above sea level) would have a horizon of almost three nautical miles. Finally, at that time these shoals were nearly awash, had small islets, and were marked by beacons – unlike the story's Tamissa Reef (Findlay 1889: 781).

Reef has gone unlocated by critics, who have taken the story's setting at face value without perceiving Conrad's alterations and inquiring what narrative purposes his departures from real-life topographies might serve. Where, then, was the true location of this reef, supposedly the site of an actual grounding that provided the model for this story's extraordinary conclusion?

There is a "Tomisa Reef" flanking the entrance to what was, in Conrad's day, the recommended passage through the Spermonde Archipelago to Makassar from the northward.[5] If this is the reef Conrad

---

Taka Bubujang, an obstruction farther away to the south, is another possible candidate for the reef on which the *Bonito*'s real-life predecessor might have been stranded. But it is "a stony patch" rather than a reef, a small, isolated shallows instead of a barrier marking the end of a channel (US *Pub. No. 163*: 181; the Admiralty chart shows the letter "r" for rocky bottom). Moreover, it was four miles from the Makassar waterfront, and in Conrad's day it would have been covered with at least 3.5 fathoms of water. A ship stranded on it giving a hull-down appearance to an observer standing in Makassar with a height of eye six feet above sea level would have required a draft of at least 21 feet and a freeboard of only a foot: unlikely dimensions for any vessel.

There is no reef south of Makassar at the distance of six or seven miles that, I estimate, would have created the sight that the townspeople notice (222). (The ease of seeing two masts with furled sails at this distance is another question; but, as I argue, this particular distance achieves a telling artistic effect independent of its actual likelihood.)

[5] Findlay writes that "there are several channels through the [Spermonde] archipelago for approaching Macassar from the northward, but the aid of a pilot is perfectly indispensable. The eastern route appears to be the best ... The northern entrance to the eastern route is marked by a *beacon* buoy, painted *black* with a *white band*, at 2 miles West of *Pani Kiang Island*" (1889: 783; italics in original).

A modern pilot guide gives this corresponding advice:

The N Channel to Ujung Pandang [Makassar] leads in a generally S direction, no more than 2.25 miles offshore … Vessels should possess local knowledge and have the sun in a position favorable for seeing discoloration before attempting to navigate the North Channel.

Pulau Panikiang [Findlay's "Pani Kiang Island"] … is a low, wooded island lying 1 mile W of the Sulawesi coast. The N entrance to the channel lies between a number of reefs extending 1.25 miles W from this island and Tomisa, a reef with a depth of 3.7m, 3 miles W. This reef is marked by a beacon.

had in mind, then the basic configuration of reef, passage, and harbour would seem more or less intact in his fictional account. But Tomisa Reef is 47 miles from Makassar, much too far away to correspond with its appearance in "Freya of the Seven Isles," and the transit through the Spermonde Archipelago was considerably more laborious and time-consuming than Conrad describes. In short, Conrad reduces a complex, 2,000 square mile region strewn with countless, incompletely charted reefs and islands to a simple passage past a single obstruction, and he moves one particular reef – the geographical feature on which the story depends – almost 50 miles to a position where none existed.

This radical alteration of topographical reality seems rather surprising given Conrad's claim that the story had a basis in history. Commentaries regularly repeat without question Conrad's account of the tale's genesis in a letter of 1911 to Edward Garnett:

> It is the story of the *Costa Rica* which was not more than five years old when I was in Singapore. The man's name was Sutton. He died in just that way ... He was just about to go home to marry a girl (of whom he used to talk to everybody and anybody) and bring her out there when his ship was run [on] a reef by the commander of a Dutch gunboat whom he had managed to offend in some way. He haunted the beach in Macassar for months and lies buried in the fort there.
>
> Only 18 months ago Charles Marris master and owner of the *Araby Maid* island-trader, came to see me ... [and] said: 'You ought to write the story of the *Costa Rica*. There's a good many of us left yet who remember Sutton.' And I said I would, before long. (4 August 1911, *CLA*: 469)

The rest of the transit to Makassar requires a dozen changes in course and passes close to numerous shoals and reefs (see US *Pub. No. 163*: 185).

The real passage is roughly 50 nautical miles long. The fictional *Neptun* takes 30 minutes to reach Makassar from Tamissa Reef at top speed, which (assuming an estimated seven miles to go) calculates to be 14 knots, a not-unheard of speed for a small steam warship of the late nineteenth century. The historical passage, on the other hand, would therefore have taken many hours to complete by a ship moving at the *Neptun*'s speed or less. (And a much slower speed was probable, given the hazards present.)

Conrad's explanation makes it sound as though the *Costa Rica*, captained by Sutton, served as the model for Jasper Allen and his *Bonito.* Biographers and critics from Jocelyn Baines (1960) onward repeat the link between the two ships, an association that, however, begins to unravel on closer inspection. The *Costa Rica* could have served as a model only in that she (like the *Bonito*) was involved in a legal dispute resulting in a celebrated court case. But this occurred in 1891, two years *after* Conrad left Singapore. A register of merchant shipping corroborates this timeline, listing that vessel as still being in service in 1890.[6] The *Costa Rica* could not have been the *Bonito*'s actual predecessor, just as Tamissa Reef was not where Conrad places it.[7]

---

[6] Conrad's visitor, Captain Carlos Marris, had commanded the *Vidar*, but not during Conrad's service in her (Page, 1986: 29). The two men possibly knew each other, or knew of each other, in Singapore (Allen, 1965: 227). In a letter to Conrad dated 18 July 1909, praising *The Mirror of the Sea* and proposing the visit Conrad records, Marris offers a different version of the events thirty years prior: "I finished up with Sail with Carpenter in Macassar in the old 'Costa Rica Packet' when he got into the big smuggling trouble with the Dutch there" (Stape and Knowles, ed., 1996: 66). Karl's and Davies' notes to Conrad's letter to Garnett offer more information on Carpenter and the *Costa Rica*, explaining that in 1891 Carpenter, then the *Costa Rica*'s captain, "was arrested by the Dutch authorities and taken to Macassar in a dispute over several casks of gin retrieved from a derelict proa" (*CL4* 469n.). Thus, the aspect of illegal trading is the part of the *Costa Rica*'s history Conrad transferred into fiction. But despite Conrad's explanation, the *Costa Rica* could not have been run aground because the Carpenter incident involved that ship after Conrad had left Singapore: *Lloyd's Register of Shipping* lists the vessel as being in service in 1890 (page COR-COU). Karl and Davies report that Sutton (not mentioned by Marris) is "otherwise unknown" (*CL4*: 469n).

[7] Resink (1961: 230, 232-33) considers both the *Costa Rica* and a separate case, heard in Palembang in 1879, involving gunrunning. He also suggests the survey ship *HMS Samarang*, accidentally towed aground by the steamship *Phlegethon* on a reef in the East Indies, as a source. That incident, however, took place in 1844, not the mid-1880s, and did not occur in the Straits of Makassar as has been commonly assumed. Resink points to the episode in Belcher's *Narrative of the Voyage of H.M.S. "Samarang"* (1: 188-89) when Belcher's vessel runs aground just outside the entrance to the Bay of Ambong, on the northern coast of Borneo. Resink locates Ambong in the Straits of Makassar, whereas Ambong Bay (Teluk Ambong) is, in fact, on the opposite side of Borneo from the Java Sea and Celebes, roughly 600 miles distance from Makassar.

To create what Conrad refers to as a single historical event, he seems to have combined details from the cases of the *Costa Rica*, the *Samarang*, and an otherwise unknown man named Sutton, moving Tomisa Reef and modifying the Spermonde Archipelago. At this point, one might reasonably ask why this attention to such recombinations in a work of fiction should matter, since all writers of fiction rearrange the factual world to suit their needs. But Conrad's efforts cannot but invite such inquiry when he remarks that an important part of the story is based on history, he alters the topographical facts, and finally attempts to deflect interest away from his fictional landscape, later describing the tale as having an "Eastern sea setting, but not too much setting" (to Warrington Dawson, 15 February 1911, *CL4*: 413).

Conrad sought to reveal what lies outside, or underneath, empirical reality; in his preface to *The Nigger of the "Narcissus,"* he defines art "as a single-minded attempt to render the highest kind of justice to the visible universe, by bringing to light the truth, manifold and one, underlying its every aspect" (vii). We might conclude that according to this formulation, artistic truths exist not only independent of visible reality, but also sometimes in spite of the constraints that mere facts might impose. But the element of factual accuracy can play a more subtle and vital role in this relationship than has been recognized. In "Freya of the Seven Isles," it turns out, Conrad reconfigures his seascape in ways that powerfully reinforce his art, turning what might be considered window-dressing into an essential part of bringing to light an artistic truth. He could not have expected his readers to be directly aware of his topographical alterations, of course. Readers are to a certain extent sensible of the ultimate results, however, for the changes Conrad undertakes help create a landscape whose contours are central to his thematic expression. His precise placement of Tamissa Reef, when closely examined, alerts us to a systematically organized topography enabling a number of significant effects.

To begin, then, with the striking connections Conrad draws between his depiction of the Seven Isles and the waters outside Makassar. Nelson's bungalow is situated on the western side of his island, very near the shore. In an important early episode, the narrator and Freya, from one of the verandahs, watch Jasper bring his brig into the cove:

> I suppose Jasper made the girl out with his long glass. What does he do? Instead of standing on for another mile and a half along the shoals and then tacking for the anchorage in a proper and seaman-like manner, he spies a gap between two disgusting old jagged reefs, puts the helm down suddenly, and shoots the brig through, with all her sails shaking and rattling, so that we could hear the racket on the verandah. (152)

Here, Conrad establishes an important spatial relationship out of the materials of the verandah and the reef-bound waters it overlooks, and a motif of movement through a stylized seascape that resonates at crucial points in the story.

First, this episode clearly foreshadows the *Bonito*'s eventual stranding on Tamissa Reef. Both Jasper's and Heemskirk's manoeuvres consist of piloting a ship through a short, narrow channel. The *Bonito* halts at the Seven Isles "with all her sails shaking and rattling," and she grounds off Makassar "with a strange, violent tremor of her mastheads" (220). Jasper habitually anchors as close as possible to the bungalow in order to see Freya from his ship; and after the stranding he takes a daily walk down the coast for the closest possible look at his brig and "her beloved form" (229). When Jasper leaves Freya for the last time, Freya watches the *Bonito* from her verandah until "the point below hid the hull of the brig from her view" (205); after the grounding, the horizon similarly conceals the ship's hull (222). These parallels are heightened by Conrad's reduction of the Spermonde Archipelago to a short passage past a reef barrier, effectively turning the Seven Isles and Makassar into mirror images. Conrad thereby provides a symmetrical geographic framing device to complement the frame of the narrator's telling of the tale. Additionally, in the configuration of land and sea deployed here, the author establishes spatial organizing principles that are key to the unfolding of the narrative.

This organization extends even to the floor plan of Nelson's bungalow. Conrad goes to considerable lengths to detail this layout. The square building has east and west verandahs, each associated with a particular exterior space. The west verandah is called the living room of the house. It is one of Freya's usual stations and overlooks the cove where Jasper carries out his ship handling feats. The east verandah, on the other hand, is the exclusive preserve of old Nelson. There, alone, he frequently sits motionless in "perplexed thinking" while facing the direction of Makassar, on whose shore Jasper will ultimately exercise his own stationary, ceaseless ruminations (182). Furthermore, "blinds of sail-cloth" contribute to the "privacy" of Nelson's verandah, corresponding to the "furled sails" that are the subject of Jasper's solitary contemplation (182, 222).

"The north verandah was not a verandah at all, really," Conrad explains. "It was more like a long balcony. It did not communicate with the other two, and could only be approached by a passage inside the house. Thus it had a privacy which made it a convenient place for a maiden's meditations without words," and also her intimate meetings with Jasper (182). The characteristics of this north balcony, what the narrator calls Freya's "boudoir," and which she outfits with furniture to make it a homey space, echo those of the private world Jasper intends to make for Freya on board the *Bonito*: "this brig was the home to be – their home – the floating paradise which he was gradually fitting out like a yacht to sail his life blissfully away in with Freya" (183, 152).

In the episode that proves the catalyst for Jasper's undoing, he and Freya are together on the north verandah. Conrad intervenes conspicuously to describe the spatial arrangement that permits what happens next. The author notes that "The interior of the bungalow was divided by two passages crossing each other in the middle," to which I would add that the two hallways symbolize Heemskirk's and Jasper's crossed desire for the same woman (184). For it is from one of these hallways that Heemskirk, passing through the house looking for the pair, chances to turn his head and see them, embracing, framed in the doorway to the verandah. This sight enrages him and plants the seeds of his revenge on Jasper. Altogether, the house's peculiar floor plan makes perfect sense as a reproduction, in interior space, of the author's rendering of both the larger physical world and the tale's psychological territory.

The action at Tamissa Reef represents a culmination of the functions of setting discussed thus far, through its particular spatial arrangement both re-enacting and resolving the situation of proximity, danger, and desire established by Jasper's physical presence in the Seven Isles. Thus the configuration of this reef and passage, while not true to history, is indispensable to the symbolic structure and artistic integrity of the work. Perhaps it was for this reason that Conrad adamantly opposed changing this story's ending when it became clear that magazine editors, reacting to the story's gloom, would not publish the tale as submitted. In response to two rejections, he somewhat famously wrote in the same letter to Garnett quoted above "As to faking a 'sunny' ending to my story I would see all the American Magazines and all the american Editors damned in heaps before lifting my pen for that task" (*CL4*: 469). Yet while Conrad resisted changing the ending to suit the readership of popular magazines, he decided to make just that concession in final revisions to his next work, *Chance*, giving it a happier conclusion specifically for its appearance in the *New York Herald* (Fraser 1996: 35).

From the very beginning, "Freya of the Seven Isles" has held a troubled position in the Conrad canon. Disliked by readers after a publication marred by false starts, the tale has generally been appraised as a flawed and weak expression of Conrad's talents. Critics have found fault in, among other things, its uneven style, sentimentality, and moral simplicity. Baines, for example, cites "occasional lapses into facetiousness or heartiness," its "extreme romanticism," and "operatic form" (1960: 376, 392). Graver emphasizes the tale's "stylistic imprecision and structural mismanagement" and the difficult-to-believe changes its characters undergo (1969: 163-65). Later appraisals tend to agree about the story's improbabilities and thin construction. But these assessments, valid as they may otherwise be, overlook the central role of the story's setting – the significance of which becomes apparent only when the fictional and factual topographies are closely compared. I suggest that Conrad's reshaping of the landscape constitutes a narrative strategy whose skillfulness offsets the weaknesses other readers have found and lends "Freya of the Seven Isles" greater depth than critics have remarked. The shortcomings of the tale's superficial structure can tend to obscure the coherent and broad reaching organizing principles embedded in the carefully arranged landscape. Taking the important role of setting into account therefore complicates previous evaluations of the story, at least with regard to its formal characteristics and its relationship to its sources, and indicates that the tale is perhaps too easily dismissed as relatively unworthy of greater critical attention. This neglected work invites a larger reconsideration that, while beyond the scope of this article, might benefit from similarly unexplored approaches.

That Conrad should alter and embroider the visible world when necessary for his artistic expression comes as no surprise. But the specific relationships between his altered setting and his artistic goals deserve to be recognized and studied as one means of gaining a fuller understanding of this deceptively simple tale. Near the story's conclusion, the narrator asks "who could associate a girl nine hundred miles away with the stranding of a ship on Tamissa reef, or look for the remote filiation of that event in the psychology of at least three people?" (222). These lines, questioning the visible world's deeper significance and recalling to us the stylized setting of the beginning and end, hint at just how much the narrative owes its power to topographical changes. The intriguing associations that the narrator finds so elusive lie hidden, I would argue, in the interpenetration of topography and psychology at the heart of this tale – where territorial vision and revision become one.

Acknowledgements

A version of this paper was presented at the Conrad and Territoriality Conference held at the University of British Columbia, Vancouver, in August 2002 in conjunction with the Joseph Conrad Society of America and with the financial support of the Social Sciences and Humanities Research Council of Canada.

Thanks are due to Basia Kielska and Steven Schimmel for assisting with translations of Polish and Dutch materials, respectively.

Works cited

Allen, Jerry. *The Sea Years of Joseph Conrad.* Garden City, NY: Doubleday, 1965.

Baines, Jocelyn. *Joseph Conrad.* New York: McGraw-Hill, 1960.

Belcher, Captain Sir Edward, *Narrative of the Voyage of H.M.S. SAMARANG, During the Years 1843-46; Employed Surveying the Islands of the Eastern Archipelago; Accompanied by a Brief Vocabulary of the Principal Languages.* 1848. Vol. 1. Rpt. Folkestone and London: Dawsons of Pall Mall, 1970.

Braun, Andrzej, and Andrzej Strumiłło. *Conrad-dotknięcie Wschodu.* Warszawa: Wydawnictwo Artystyczno-Graficzne, 1970.

British Admiralty. *China Sea: Celebes: Approach to Makassar: Chart No. 1293.* London: Hydrographic Office, 1898. Large corrections up to 1899.

———. *China Sea: Banka Strait to Singapore: Chart No. 2757.* London: Hydrographic Office, 1861. Large corrections up to 1897; small corrections up to 1900.

Findlay, Alexander G. *A Directory for the Navigation of the Indian Archipelago, and the Coast of China, from the Straits of Malacca and Sunda, and the Passages East of Java, to Canton, Shanghai, the Yellow Sea, and Korea, with Descriptions of the Winds, Monsoons, and Currents, and General Instructions for the Various Channels, Harbours, etc.* 3rd edn. London: Richard Holmes Laurie, 1889.

Fraser, Gail. "The Short Fiction." *The Cambridge Companion to Joseph Conrad.* Ed. J. H. Stape. Cambridge: Cambridge University Press, 1996. 25-44.

Graver, Lawrence. *Conrad's Short Fiction.* Berkeley: University of California, 1969.

Lloyd's Register of Shipping. *Lloyd's Register of British and Foreign Shipping: Established 1834, United with the Underwriter's Registry for Iron Vessels in 1885, From 1st July, 1890, to the 30th June, 1891.* London: Lloyd's Register, 1890.

Marris, Carlos M. Letter to Joseph Conrad of 18 July 1909. In *A Portrait in Letters: Correspondence to and about Conrad.* 66-68. Ed. J. H. Stape and Owen Knowles. Amsterdam-Atlanta: Rodopi, 1996.

Page, Norman. *A Conrad Companion.* London: Macmillan, 1986.

Resink, G. J. "Jozef Korzeniowski's Voornaamste Lectuur Betreffende Indonesië." *Bijdragen tot de taal-, land- en volkenkunde* 117 (1961): 209-37.

Sherry, Norman. *Conrad's Eastern World.* Cambridge: Cambridge University Press, 1966.

United States, Defense Mapping Agency, *Pub No. 163: Sailing Directions (Enroute): Borneo, Jawa, Sulawesi, and Nusa Tenggara.* 7th ed. Bethesda, MD: DMA, 1996.

Conrad and the Erotic: “A Smile of Fortune” and “The Planter of Malata”

Jeremy Hawthorn
Norwegian University of Science and Technology, Trondheim

SINCE THOMAS C. MOSER'S *Joseph Conrad: Achievement and Decline* appeared in 1957, discussion of the sharply varying quality of Conrad's fiction and analysis of his depiction of relationships between men and women seem destined to overlap. Moser's diagnosis of what he considers the debilitating sickness in Conrad's fiction is neither simple nor simplistic but involves a clear thesis: “love” is “the lowest common denominator of the apprentice work … of the inferior short novels … of the weak portions of “Heart of Darkness,” *Lord Jim*, and *Nostromo*.” It also “dominates the later period, where it is central to six of the seven novels” (3-4). Moser concludes that the “sympathetic treatment of love between a white man and a woman is not congenial to the early Conrad's creativity” (65).

In such summarizing statements Moser blames Conrad's attempt to write about love, not about sexuality, for inadequacies in the better work and for his “decline.” But his account of the relationship between love and sexuality in Conrad, between, say, the romantic and the erotic, is not always as clear as one might wish. Discussing “The Return,” for example, which he characterizes as “a bad piece of writing,” he writes that it provides a “*locus classicus* for the near paralysis of Conrad's creativity when dealing with a sexual subject,” and that “it is significant that Conrad's one extended study of a sexual subject should center in an inadequate male who sees female sexuality as an inescapable menace” (1957: 77). In contrast, he enthusiastically describes “A Smile of Fortune” as “a first-rate story of female sexuality and male impotence” (98).

That critics still engage with Moser's thesis says something about its importance, but it has had unfortunate after-effects. Susan Jones's complaint that "the neglect of Conrad's interest in writing for and about women has been perpetuated by a bifurcation of his work into eras of decline and achievement" (1999: 222) is representative of misgivings. Moser's book also unfortunately gave rise to the view that Conrad could not write well about sexuality or the erotic. At one point Moser states baldly that "Conrad differs radically from other great modern novelists in his lack of understanding, in his almost belligerent lack of genuine, dramatic interest in sexual problems" (1957: 128). One might wonder how someone with such a "belligerent" lack of interest in sexual problems, and whose creativity suffered near paralysis when dealing with sexuality, could have written a first-rate story of female sexuality and male impotence – just when his decline was imminent.

Conrad's work is not naturally associated with the "erotic." The word itself occurs only once in his writings, in Part Two, Chapter 3 of *Chance*: Captain Anthony is the son of "a delicate erotic poet of a markedly refined and autocratic temperament" (309). The mention is not without interest, given that the erotic is linked with power in a passage that may well have been drafted at about the time the two stories considered here were written. A concern with the erotic does not, of course, depend on use of the word.

Both in his lifetime and after his death, Conrad, as Susan Jones points out in *Conrad and Women*, has often been thought of as a writer whose male characters perform centre-stage while his female ones are present on the periphery or in the wings. There is a common view that his romantic and potentially erotic scenes too often slide into the melodramatic, and for modern readers few things are less erotic. Moments of passion or sexual excitement are rare, and often presented in such a way as to minimize or remove any evocation of the erotic in the reader. Sometimes they are combined with conventionalised or clichéd depictions of the "exotic" as in *An Outcast of the Islands* or "The Lagoon." At times they occur "offstage," recalled only through signs and tokens as in the glimpse of Hollis's mementoes in "Karain." At other times they are presented in distanced, even darkly humorous ways, as in the mutual attraction between Falk and Hermann's niece in *Falk*. And where another writer might have evoked a sense of sexual attraction between Jim and Jewel, Conrad displays no interest. Even so, flashes of erotic excitement are depicted and enacted in several works. Some of the more interesting, such as in "The Secret Sharer" and *The Shadow-Line* – and perhaps *Lord Jim* – involve the homoerotic. But other works display and analyse the erotic from a male heterosexual perspective, and this essay devotes particular attention to one – "A Smile of Fortune" (1911). Moreover, as writing about love was, as Moser claimed, the main reason why Conrad's fiction "declined," I wish to set this novella alongside "The Planter of Malata," written three years later. My overall aim is to explore an undervalued aspect of Conrad's writing – its depiction and analysis of the erotic – and to reconsider the nature, or even existence, of Conrad's "decline."

Critical assessments of "A Smile of Fortune" and "The Planter of Malata" have been mixed.[1] The former, I think, is one of Conrad's finest short fictions, while the latter is a failure, mainly of interest to the literary pathologist. "A Smile of Fortune" was the first work Conrad produced after the three-month convalescence subsequent to his breakdown after completing *Under Western Eyes*, the work that Moser and others see as his final major "achievement" in the novel. This, along with the fact that the novella is concerned with its young captain-narrator's abortive sexual obsession with a young woman, might lead us to expect the story to serve as copybook example of Conrad's decline, if only in incipient or partial form. To the extent that the work can be taken to be Conrad at his near-best it serves rather as a copybook example of the awkward limb that sticks out of the Procrustean bed of the thesis that when Conrad turned to matters of love and sexuality his writing suffered.

---

[1] Critical responses to "A Smile of Fortune" are generally more positive than those to "The Planter of Malata," but both works have prompted wildly varying judgements. These range, in the case of the first, from Thorburn's view that in *'Twixt Land and Sea Tales* "so fine a story as 'The Secret Sharer' is framed by the embarrassing operatics of 'A Smile of Fortune' and 'Freya of the Seven Isles'" (1974: 22) to Watts's view that the story is "one of Conrad's most brilliant yet most neglected and under-rated works" (1985: 131). Said describes "The Planter" (with considerable reservations, it is true) as "Conrad's most pessimistic story, and a masterpiece nevertheless" (1966: 162), while Knowles praises it as "one of the most interesting and problematic failures among Conrad's novellas" (1979: 177). Erdinast-Vulcan argues that the "artistic failure of ['The Planter'] is due to a large extent to the failure of the initial framing strategy" (1999: 162), a suggestion taken up later in this essay.

In brief, the argument here is that while "A Smile of Fortune" is a Modernist work in which sexuality and the erotic are conceptualised and understood in ways appropriate to modernity and informed by the insights of contemporary understanding, sexuality in "The Planter of Malata" is understood and depicted in terms of an anachronistically melodramatic outlook.

The earlier story sees desire and the erotic inextricably connected to class, power, and violence, much as Freud has led us to expect in the modern age. In "The Planter of Malata," in contrast, sexuality and desire are mediated through courtly-love and fairy-tale conventions that involve self-sacrifice, chastity, and knightly devotion. Because these are not of the time *in* which or *about* which Conrad is writing, they prevent his making contact with the erotic as he or his contemporaries lived it. *Chance*, whose latter part was written at about the same as these stories, involves *both* a chivalric and courtly-love element (seen strongly in its chapter titles) *and* a Modernist element, in its engagement with feminism, lesbianism, and hints of sadistic arousal. Separating out these elements into two very different stories allows us to perceive the Modernist element's strength and the chivalric one's weakness.

The settings of both stories owe much to a brief period of Conrad's life. If not an *annus mirabilis*, 1888 provided him with experiences that he used in several works written at different points in his career. Notably, many of his fictions containing an erotic element have some connection with this period. Appointed Master of the *Otago* in January, Conrad sailed from Bangkok on 9 February to Singapore and then on to Sydney, arriving in the Australian capital on 7 May. After a return voyage to Melbourne, he sailed to Port-Louis, Mauritius on 7 August, staying for seven weeks after his arrival on 30 September. "The Planter of Malata" opens in a "great colonial city," which the manuscript identifies as Sydney, while the "Pearl of the Ocean" of "A Smile of Fortune" is clearly modelled on Mauritius.[2]

Both stories trace the history of solitary but active and independent young men who become obsessed with a woman while dealing with complications in which the woman's father is involved. In both

---

[2] See entries in Knowles and Moore (2000) on "A Smile of Fortune," "The Planter of Malata," "Australia," and "Mauritius."

stories the father seems anxious that the relationship be legitimately consummated. In both cases, the young man initiates passionate physical contact, only for the relationship to end in separation, and in the case of "The Planter of Malata" in death. Both works, in short, deal with the sort of male heterosexual fixation and obsession that can easily become the stuff of melodrama but can also be analysed in terms of contemporary understandings of sexuality.

A Smile of Fortune

If both stories owe much to Conrad's experiences in 1888, "A Smile of Fortune" is linked to that year by more compelling textual evidence. This story details the captain-narrator's growing obsession with the young Alice Jacobus. (According to the captain's informant, the eldest brother of one of the old French families, "She must be over eighteen now" [38]). Alice is the illegitimate daughter of the merchant and ship's chandler Alfred Jacobus, who although married, ran off with a female circus-rider who became Alice's mother. Because of her scandalous origins Jacobus keeps his daughter in social and physical seclusion, confined to the house and its suggestively luxuriant walled garden. Looked after by "an elderly female relative" (38), who serves as her *gouvernante*, she gleans what she knows of the world from "newspapers provided for the captains' room of the 'store'" and brought home "in a very stained and ragged condition" (60). (Both "A Smile of Fortune" and "The Planter of Malata" share a contemptuous attitude to journalism and the press, though they are far from the only works in Conrad's canon to have this in common.)

In 1888, newspapers did not lack for sensational copy: "At that time the batches of papers brought by the last mail reported a series of crimes in the East End of London, there was a sensational case of abduction in France and a fine display of armed robbery in Australia" (61). The "series of crimes in the East End of London" must be the "Ripper" murders of autumn 1888. Ned Kelly's armed robberies occurred earlier: he was hanged in 1880. Such a diet of reading forms Alice's view of the world-at-large: "she had formed for herself a notion of the civilised world as a scene of murders, abductions, burglaries, stabbing affrays, and every sort of desperate violence" (60). Thus when the "elderly female relative" remarks: "I don't know what your precious papa is plotting with that fellow. But he's just the sort of man who's capable of carrying you off far away somewhere and then cutting your throat some day for your money" (61), Alice takes the warning seriously, and the captain's position is not helped by the fact that she perceives no irony in his response:

> "Yes, that's what we do with girls in Europe," I began in a grimly matter-of-fact tone. I think Miss Jacobus was disconcerted by my sudden appearance. I turned upon her with cold ferocity:
>
> "As to objectionable old women, they are first strangled quietly, then cut up into small pieces and thrown away, a bit here and a bit there. They vanish – " (62)

Conrad's earliest surviving reference to "A Smile of Fortune" comes in a letter to John Galsworthy of 17 May 1910, in which he announces: "I am going to begin to morrow a short story.... It's to be comical in a nautical setting and its subject is (or *are*) potatoes. Title: A Smile of Fortune" (*CL4*: 329). The reader is invited to find passages such as that just quoted "comical," but only later does the reader discover that Alice firmly believes that the captain and her father are planning her abduction (or worse), and that she is, literally, terrified. Ted Billy has described "A Smile of Fortune" as a "seriocomic romance" (1997: 88), and throughout the story references to violent and tragic events are juxtaposed with humorous and comic elements: at the opening a bereaved captain mourning his son gives way to a bereaved captain ludicrously mourning the loss of his ship's figurehead. Nonetheless, this is a story that includes very dark elements that Conrad's humour repeatedly obscures or displaces. The one I wish to draw attention to is that of the captain's alternate (or even simultaneous) masochistic and sadistic arousal by Alice's expression of both contempt and fear for him.

If Conrad's memory of his time Mauritius in 1888 and his romantic involvements with one and perhaps two young women constitute a basis of personal experience from which he constructed "A Smile of Fortune," it is noteworthy that writing the story twenty-two years later he also recalled that at that time the papers were full of reports of the "Ripper" murders – and perhaps, too, of a French abduction, and an Australian armed robbery. Very soon after he began writing the novella the Dr Crippen murder case broke in the British press, and Conrad was asked by the *Daily Mail*'s literary editor to review the books that Crippen had with him on the *Montrose*, which the fugitive boarded with his mistress Ethel le Neve at Antwerp, bound for Quebec (Ray, ed., 1990: 63).[3]

During both the time *about which* and *at which* Conrad was writing "A Smile of Fortune," the newspapers were full of reports of a violent murderer who killed one or more women.[4] Violence to women does not merely lurk at the text's borders: in the newspapers Alice reads, it spills into the text and sensitises readers to a continued suggestion that male heterosexual desire in the story is linked sadistically and masochistically to pain, fear, and humiliation. When Alice first sets eyes on the captain, he reports that "Under her amazement there was a hint of fear, and then came a flash as of anger" (43). These two responses – fear and anger – appear to have erotic force for the captain. As his obsessive need to visit Alice deepens from day to day, the captain attempts to distinguish between her reality as a person independent of himself, and his puzzled, if not tormented, awareness of his desire for her:

> I was looking at the girl. It was what I was coming for daily; troubled, ashamed, eager; finding in my nearness to her a unique sensation which I indulged with dread, self-contempt, and deep pleasure, as if it were a secret vice bound to end in

---

[3] Summarized in Ray, ed., 1990: 64-65, the story is from Archibald Marshall's *Out and About: Random Reminiscences* (London: Murray, 1933, p.145). In Ray's report, Crippen was arrested in Canada [1910], and Marshall was sent a list of the books that he had read on the voyage. He invited Conrad to write an article about Crippen's "sea library," but "poor dear Conrad exploded in epistolary fury at being asked to do such a thing and severed his connection with our journal" (in Ray, ed., 1990: 65).

[4] Stephen Donovan has drawn my attention to a comparable passage in *The Arrow of Gold* in which the narrator is surprised by Therese's nervousness but explains that "there had been ... a case of atrocious murder," and that even though Therese did not read the papers she could not avoid hearing of it. The passage goes on to detail the narrator's chaffing of Therese about the many murderers in the house – to which teasing she responds in kind, rather as Alice's *gouvernante* does (138-39).

> my undoing, like the habit of some drug or other which ruins and degrades its slave. (62)

What is it about his desire that he associates with "dread, self-contempt, and deep pleasure"? How is his attraction comparable to a drug habit?[5] Soon after this passage, Alice asks him why he keeps on "coming here." The captain's response to himself is at least honest: "I could not have told her. I could not even tell myself with sincerity why I was coming there" (63). What is that "strange, half-evil, half-tender sensation which had given its acrid flavour to so many days, which had made her appear tragic and promising, pitiful and provoking" (78) and that disappears during his final meeting with Alice?

In the captain's attempts to come to terms with, and to isolate and understand, his desire, is a recurrent yoking together of opposites: self-contempt and deep pleasure; half-evil, half-tender, "tragic and promising, pitiful and provoking" (78). At the heart of this contradiction-filled desire lies his shameful perception of the contradictory nature of his attraction to Alice, an attraction sadistically fuelled by her fear and by his perception of her vulnerability and his potential power over her, and masochistically by her contempt for and indifference to him. On the narrative's surface, the captain is presented as a kind man, heartily shocked and disgusted by Ernest Jacobus's violent bullying of his unacknowledged mulatto son. But under the surface – both of the captain's depicted self-awareness and of the narrative's tracing of his relations with Alice – the captain recognizes a guilty pleasure in his sense of power over Alice, in his realization that he inspires fear in her, that he has the power to hurt her, and is, indeed, doing just that. If the two Jacobus brothers represent sadism and masochism, the respectable and the outcast, the captain's confusion of Ernest and Alfred indicates that contrary impulses are to be found in his make-up.

If this sounds unlike Conrad, it is worth remembering that "A Smile of Fortune" is not his only work to associate male heterosexual

---

[5] Stephen Donovan has suggested to me that the captain's "daily" dose of "sensation" can be compared to Alice's reading of the sensational stories in the dailies. In such a reading, sexuality is no longer an unchanging biological force but a biological impulse mediated through culturally distinct institutions, experiences, and expectations.

excitement with perverse or perverted pleasure. In *Chance*, half-finished at the time "A Smile of Fortune" was written, the first meeting between Captain Anthony and Flora – during which Anthony saves Flora from committing suicide – is replete with strong indications that the captain is erotically aroused by Flora's suffering and his sense of power over her:

> What seemed most awful to her was the elated light in his eyes, the rapacious smile that would come and go on his lips as if he were gloating over her misery. But her misery was his opportunity and he rejoiced while the tenderest pity seemed to flood his own being. … It was obvious the world had been using her ill. And even as he spoke with indignation the very marks and stamp of this ill-usage of which he was so certain seemed to add to the inexplicable attraction he felt for her person. It was not pity alone, I take it. It was something more spontaneous, perverse and exciting. (223-24)

"Spontaneous, perverse and exciting": the emotions explored at this point in *Chance* are very close to those charted and investigated in "A Smile of Fortune."

In one of the tale's deepest ironies, the captain's sexual obsession with Alice is revealed as part inverted mirror-image, part duplicate, of Alfred Jacobus's ignominious pursuit of the circus horseback-rider. As Jerome Zuckerman puts it: "the narrator's plight comes to parallel that of Jacobus, an indication of the partnership that develops between them and their mutual weakness and guilt. Just as Jacobus' passion had enslaved him to the circus-rider, so now the captain becomes helpless in his passion for Alice" (1964: 100). If Alfred seems to derive a perverted masochistic pleasure from being humiliated by the object of his desire, the captain's secret vice has sadistic and masochistic aspects. The captain presents Alfred Jacobus's degrading obsession with the circus-rider as clearly "Other," as unlike himself, but the fascination the story exerts on his imagination warns that his attempt to distance himself from Jacobus's humiliation is only partly convincing:

> He followed that woman to the Cape, and apparently travelled at the tail of that beastly circus to other parts of the world, in a most degrading position. The woman soon ceased to care for him, and treated him worse than a dog. Most

> extraordinary stories of moral degradation were reaching the island at that time. …
>
> The grotesque image of a fat, pushing ship-chandler, enslaved by an unholy love-spell, fascinated me … (36)

The captain's condescending contempt turns out to be premature: later he has recourse to words similar to those used here to represent Alfred Jacobus's passion, in order to describe his own sexual obsession for Alfred's daughter Alice: "It was like being the slave of some depraved habit" (59); "like the habit of some drug or other which ruins and degrades its slave" (62). If the circus-rider treated Alfred "worse than a dog"– the captain is told of "the depth of passion under that placid surface, which even cuts with a riding-whip[6] (so the legend had it) could never ruffle into the semblance of a storm'" (56) – the captain realizes with "sudden dismay" that "I would be no longer able to come into this verandah, sit on this chair, and taste perversely the flavour of contempt in her indolent poses, drink in the provocation of her scornful looks, and listen to the curt, insolent remarks uttered in that harsh and seductive voice" (65).

Whereas Alfred Jacobus sticks by his circus-rider and even, apparently, plots to ensnare the captain into marrying his daughter, the captain deserts Alice at the point at which his desire dies and she appears before him as an independent individual. Why? The implied answer is that whereas the circus-rider continues to treat Jacobus with contempt, feeding and satisfying his masochistic impulses, Alice rids herself, first, of her fear of the captain and, some time later, of her contempt for, or indifference to, him. At this point, when he has to deal with her as an equal interested in and attracted to him, his desire evaporates. For the captain, it would appear, equality is not erotic.

---

[6] Stephen Donovan has pointed out to me that in November 1909, Winston Churchill was sensationally "horsewhipped" by a Suffragette ("cut with a whip" is probably more accurate). A letter from Conrad to John Galsworthy of the 15 November, 1909, comments at length on a story in the issue of the *Standard* that discusses the incident (*CL4*: 288-90). The link between the whipping of a man by a woman and the Suffrage Movement is thought-provoking, given that *Chance* is occupied with the wider issue of women's rights.

About two-thirds through the story, when the captain tells Alice that he will set sail the next day, "She murmured a distinctly scared 'So soon,' and getting up quickly, went to the little table and poured herself a glass of water." As Alice walks past him with "rapid steps and with an indolent swaying of her whole young figure above the hips" the captain feels "with tenfold force the charm of the peculiar, promising sensation I had formed the habit to seek near her" (64-65). He has to exercise sudden self-control to prevent himself from "jumping up to stride about, shout, gesticulate, make her a scene" and realizes that "It was just the relief of violence that I wanted," although outwardly he attempts to keep his lips in a "half-indulgent, half-mocking smile which was my shield against the shafts of her contempt and the insulting sallies flung at me by the old woman" (65). The key words here are "scared" and "violence" (his sadistic desire) and "contempt" (his masochistic desire). This is not the first time he entertains a fantasy of treating Alice violently; in an early scene his frustration with her leads him to feel "as if I could have done her some violence – shaken her, beaten her maybe" (54). If this enslavement by Alice's fear, on the one hand, and indolence and contempt, on the other, this drinking-in of her provocatively scornful looks and seductively curt and insolent remarks, merit the verdict of "perverse," with its shadowy hint of "perverted," the captain's full "perversity" becomes most apparent at that point of the tale that has typically surprised the first-time reader of the novella: his sudden loss of desire.

Moser focuses attention on to the captain's changing interest. First, he characterizes this interest as voyeuristic: "Since Alice seldom speaks to the captain and since she usually has a chaperone in attendance, his desire for her seems, as he says, "unrealizable." In fact, he wants it that way. He comes only to *look* at her in her thin wrapper that reveals a "young supple body" (1957: 97). He justifies his diagnosis by referring to the passage from already quoted ("I was looking … slave" [62]), then goes on to argue that "Simply looking at Alice sufficiently satisfies the young captain, until she shows her indifference. This is such a blow to his vanity that he desires her, in order to prove his manhood" (98). If we return to Conrad's text, however, neither claim can be justified. The captain does *not* simply want to look at Alice; he wants to satisfy his sadistic and masochistic tendencies by enjoying her fear and contempt, and his desire starts well before she becomes indifferent to him. Moser is right, however, that the story is able to delve deeply and analytically into the captain's sexuality by tracing the stages through which his desire progresses. In particular, the captain's sudden loss of desire, a heretofore so powerfully obsessive force, is especially significant: this loss is the final stage in a sequence of rapid alterations in the nature of the relationship between the captain and Alice.

The first of these alterations comes after the captain has solemnly promised Alice that he will do nothing to her, nor will he allow her father to force him to harm her. On this declaration, her behaviour is transformed:

> To watch the change in the girl was like watching a miracle – the gradual but swift relaxation of her tense glance, of her stiffened muscles, of every fibre of her body. That black, fixed stare into which I had read a tragic meaning more than once, in which I had found a sombre seduction, was perfectly empty now, void of all consciousness whatever, and not even aware any longer of my presence; …
>
> But, man being a perverse animal, instead of rejoicing at my complete success, I beheld it with astounded and indignant eyes. (68)

The captain's perverse indignation is the result of his loss of power to inspire dread in Alice, now "not even aware any longer of my presence." He derives no sadistic pleasure from observing her fear, but does not yet lose his desire: he can still derive masochistic pleasure from her contempt. But when both fear *and* contempt disappear to be replaced by her romantic interest in him, he, perversely, loses interest in her.

Three things are necessary for the captain's desire to evaporate: first, she must cease to be afraid of him; second she must cease being contemptuous of, or indifferent to, him; and, finally, she must take the initiative in encouraging romantic contact. If her fear satisfies his sadistic impulses and her contempt and indifference are productive of a masochistic pleasure, her genuine romantic interest in him as an equal leaves him cold. For the captain, it would appear, the romantic without the exercise of power is not erotic.

When it is merely a matter of Alice's being indifferent to him, the captain witnesses her "revelling contemptuously in a sense of relief, easing her limbs in freedom after all these days of crouching, motionless poses when she had been so furious and so afraid," acting "with supreme indifference, incredible, offensive, exasperating, like ingratitude doubled with treachery," and offering "to pass by me as if I were a wooden post or a piece of furniture." At this point he attempts to replace her indifference with a new version of the superior-subservient relationship: he places both arms round her waist, "and the first kiss I planted on her closed lips was vicious enough to have been a bite" (69).

At this point Alice is transformed for the captain: "I felt her there, close against me, young, full of vigour, of life, a strong desirable creature, but as if she did not care in the least, in the absolute assurance of her safety, what I did or left undone" (69). After she escapes from him, he is confounded, hesitating between violence and love: "I could not make up my mind whether to shake my fist in that direction or blow a kiss" (70). The close relationship between the erotic and physical violence may remind us of the scene towards the end of *The Secret Agent* which culminates in Verloc's death at his wife's hands. Verloc asks Winnie to "Come here," in "a peculiar tone, which might have been the tone of brutality, but was intimately known to Mrs. Verloc as the note of wooing" (196-97).[7]

Alice's "vigour" and "life" do not attract the captain's desire. Indeed, her subsequent display of interest in him finally kills it. For if this moment of her indecision ends the tale's fifth section, the following one opens with the captain's awareness that Alice's father has observed his

---

[7] The juxtaposition resembles one in *Victory*, when Ricardo, discovering Lena "utterly unconscious, exposed and defenceless," muses about what to do to her: "Ravish or kill – it was all one to him" (288). Drawing on Bagnall, Hampson (2001) convincingly supports the claim that the alert reader is meant to recognize Ricardo as Jack the Ripper. He also argues persuasively that the author of the "rather summary recollections of an Assistant Commissioner of Police" that Conrad mentions in his Author's Note to *The Secret Agent* – actually Dr Robert Anderson, whose *Sidelights on the Home Rule Movement* was published in 1906 – could have provided Conrad with tantalizing information about the Ripper mystery in other writings, including an article in *Blackwood's Magazine* of March 1910, two months before Conrad's first extant reference to "A Smile of Fortune." However that may be, Conrad's imagination seems to have been much exercised by the brutal association of sexuality, violence, and murder provided in the Ripper case.

sexual wrestling. The next time he meets Alice, she appears not when he calls for her but some time afterwards:

> The girl, when I turned my head at a slight noise, appeared to me very tall and slender, advancing with a swaying limp, a floating and uneven motion which ended in the sinking of her shadowy form into the deep low chair. And I don't know why or whence I received the impression that she had come too late. She ought to have appeared at my call. She ought to have . . . It was as if a supreme opportunity had been missed. (76-77)

This is a small but crucial detail: "She ought to have appeared at my call." She has displayed her independence of him. In the lines that follow the captain discovers that his desire has vanished:

> "If you buttoned the strap you would not be losing your shoe, Miss Don't Care,"[8] I said, trying to be playful without conviction. I felt more like wailing over the lost illusion of vague desire, over the sudden conviction that I would never find again near her the strange, half-evil, half-tender sensation which had given its acrid flavour to so many days, which had made her appear tragic and promising, pitiful and provoking. That was all over. (77-78)

Once his ability to make her afraid or to bathe in her contempt has evaporated and the captain has to face Alice as a sexual equal, his desire evaporates: "That was all over."

The Crippen case involved not simply a wife's murder but Crippen's obsession with a younger woman who fled with him dressed

---

[8] My maternal grandmother, not much younger than the real Alice Shaw or fictional Alice Jacobus, responded to the phrase "don't care" with the saw: "Don't care didn't care: don't care was hanged," from a standard nursery rhyme. The variant familiar to my colleague Paul Goring, also imparted to him by a grandmother, is: "Don't care didn't care | Don't care was hung | Don't care was put in a bag | Until he was done." The captain's search for bags may be more significant than has been appreciated, although written variants have "boiled in a pot" rather than "put in a bag."

as a boy.[9] Alice Jacobus, like Natalia Haldin in *Under Western Eyes*, is characterized by a certain "masculinity." She has a "fine, somewhat masculine hand" (63), and her "attitude, like certain tones of her voice, had in it something masculine" (65). The captain, in contrast, when presented with flowers by Alfred Jacobus, "assured him jocularly … that he made me feel as if I were a pretty girl, and that he mustn't be surprised if I blushed" (22-23). The episode prepares for the challenge to his sense of his masculinity that awaits the captain in the fertile and seductive garden from which these flowers have been picked, and, taken together, these different episodes prepare for a narrative in which any conventional belief that gender roles and identities are allotted unproblematically on the basis of sex is likely to be challenged and undermined.[10] Early in the story the captain is told of the dispute between the two Jacobus brothers by "the chief clerk" who talks "primly," walks "mincingly," and "resembled an old maid … shocked by some impropriety" (14). As with the effeminate Chief Steward in *The Shadow-Line*, the early introduction of this character prepares for a world in which sexual identity does not guarantee conventional gender characteristics. Monika Elbert has pointed out that "A Smile of Fortune" is "a harbor story, a liminal setting which collapses boundaries between feminine and masculine" (2001: 139), and

---

[9] In a letter to John Galsworthy of 5 August 1910, Conrad reported that he had written 14,000 words of "A Smile of Fortune" and expected that another 6,000 would finish it. (The story in Dent's Collected Edition is 25,655 words long.) A letter to E. L. Sanderson of 2 September 1910 states that the story is "just finished" (*CL4*: 364). The arrest warrant for Crippen was issued on 16 July, and he and his mistress arrested in Quebec at the end of July, when Conrad was asked to review Crippen's library for the *Daily Mail* (see note above). Crippen's trial began on 18 October 1910; he was executed on 23 November. Thus while Conrad was writing the second half of "A Smile of Fortune" (including his comment about what is done to "objectionable old women" in Europe) newspapers were full of the discovery of a body in Crippen's house and of Crippen's flight and arrest. Even had Conrad not read these, his attention would have been drawn to the murder and arrest by the request to write on Crippen's "library." Thus both in 1888 and in 1910 the newspapers would have brought to his attention the link between sexuality and male violence to women.

[10] Roberts's *Conrad and Masculinity* (2000) and *Conrad and Gender* (ed., 1993) contain valuable material on the work of a writer who once was comfortably believed to be concerned with a straightforward and unproblematic masculinity.

there is certainly a sense in which the harbour functions as a sort of border country in which conventional attributes and behaviour – including those associated with sex and gender – can be modified. The title *'Twixt Land and Sea*, the collection in which the story was published, may well puzzle: if the sea meets the land, then there is nothing between them. But perhaps "land" and "sea" are not absolute, all-embracing terms; perhaps there are areas such as the harbour that are both land and sea; and perhaps there is also an area *'Twixt Man and Woman* in which more of us live more of the time than is generally admitted.

This questioning of gender boundaries parallels the way in which other binaries are seen to be less precise and more fluid than conventionally expected. The *Hilda*'s captain mourns his wooden figure-head as much as the *Stella*'s mourns the death of a flesh-and-blood child, and the flesh-and-blood captain-narrator, amazed when the aged *gouvernante* suggests that Alice put on a corset and petticoat, asks himself: "Was I of no more account than a wooden dummy?" (48). (I have already referred to the subsequent passage in which the captain expresses his anger at Alice's "movement to pass by me as if I were a wooden post or a piece of furniture.") In the fourth paragraph the captain reports that, faced by the seductive beauty of the "Pearl of the Ocean," "horrid thoughts of business interfered with my enjoyment of an accomplished passage" (3-4), and as commentators have noted, it proves impossible for the captain, and for the reader, to separate out Alfred Jacobus's business interests from his desire to marry off his daughter. Is his daughter a tool to entrap the captain into unwanted "trading," or is the forced purchase of potatoes merely the second-best conclusion to a plot aimed at the captain's single status rather than his pocket? Is the garden in which Alice is confined a prison or an Edenic retreat from the world? (It is potatoes rather than the traditional, if unbiblical, apple that the cunning Jacobus persuades the captain to take from the paradise, but Conrad would have known that "potato" in French is *pomme de terre*: the potato seems an appropriate earthly variant of the Edenic fruit.) Is Alice herself victim or tormenter? Was her father the circus-rider's victim or a willing participant in his savoured degradation?

That neat distinction between Alfred Jacobus's apparently masochistic obsession with the circus-rider, and the captain's incipient drawing of sadistic pleasure from Alice's fear, a distinction that might underwrite the captain's claim to a manliness based on power, must be set against scenes in which the captain appears fascinated and aroused by the young woman's contempt:

> "Surely, Miss Alice, you will not let them drive me out into the street?"
>
> Her magnificent black eyes, narrowed, long in shape, swept over me with an indefinable expression, then in a harsh, contemptuous voice she let fall in French a sort of explanation:
>
> "*C'est papa.*" (45-46)

It seems appropriate that Alice's contempt is linked here to her mention of her father. At the start of the fifth section the captain reports of his relationship with Alfred Jacobus that "A sort of shady, intimate understanding seemed to have been established between us" (51), an understanding that may involve their shared knowledge of the captain's obsession with Alice, or their shared understanding of the masochistic pleasure to be derived from being badly treated by the object of such an obsession. If at the novella's opening the captain wishes to preserve boundaries – flowers should not be grown on board as salt water may rot them – by the end he recognizes the inevitable untidiness of the world and of our relations to it.

This blurring of binaries leads both the captain and the reader to recognize that the world is not a place of things susceptible to neat categorization. What makes "A Smile of Fortune" such a rich work is that there is nothing programmatic in the portrayal or analysis of the captain's desire. Among other things, it is presented as deeply intertwined with class – not as such but as a locus of power. If the novella, as has been suggested, is based on Conrad's entanglement with two women in Mauritius – the 26-year-old Eugénie Renouf, and the 17-year-old Alice Shaw – then their very different social status may have contributed to the novella's insistence on Alice's scandalously unrespectable status as the daughter of an "outcast" father and "Gipsy" mother. "A Smile of Fortune" certainly suggests that there may be an inverse relationship between social status and sexual attractiveness, not least through the foregrounded hints that Alice, with her repeatedly missing shoe or slipper, is a sort of Cinderella. Referring to the island's "old French families" (to one of which Eugénie Renouf belonged), the captain scornfully reports that the girls "are almost always pretty, ignorant of the world, kind and agreeable and generally bilingual; they prattle innocently both in French and English. The emptiness of their existence passes belief" (34-35).

During his sojourn in Mauritius it appears that Conrad proposed to Eugénie Renouf only to discover that she was engaged.[11] Such an experience can hardly have other than humiliating, and it would not have been surprising had that humiliation resulted in an anger that sought emotional revenge or at least the refuge of a relationship in which the woman was humiliated. Such speculation is just that, but offers a plausible biographical source for the mingled masochistic and sadistic impulses that Alice Jacobus inspires in the captain and that he finds so erotically enslaving.

Alice Shaw did not belong to one of these families, and research has uncovered the fact that her father, a shipping agent, owned the island's only rose garden.[12] The story's Alice is described as having the "dishevelled magnificent hair of a gipsy tramp" (59), and the captain – doubtless alluding to the now-discredited belief that gypsies are of Egyptian origin, as the etymology suggests – claims that she had found her "long, Egyptian eyes" in the sawdust of the circus (71). If we accept the suggestion that this "harbour story" offers a liminal setting in which established conventions can be thrown off and alternative forms of behaviour tested, then the carnivalesque associations of the circus attached to the circus-rider and to Alice, her daughter, are entirely appropriate.

"Heart of Darkness" sets the sterile and bloodless European Intended against Kurtz's fecund, energetic, and sexual African mistress. Alice Jacobus combines the characteristics of these two matched or contrasted characters. On the one hand, she is an isolated young European woman, ignorant of the world; on the other hand, she is associated with the suggestively luxuriant forces of nature within her father's walled garden. Certainly her bodily reality is set against the socially correct but unbelievably empty existences of the island's respectable women. Her

---

[11] For a summary of Conrad's contact with Eugénie Renouf, see Najder 1983: 107-109.

[12] Najder, citing an article by P. J. Barnwell about Conrad in the *Dictionary of Mauritian Biography*, describes Alice Shaw's father as a shipping-agent (1983: 522 n. 76). Baines calls him "a stevedore" (1960: 128).

clothing suggests rather than conceals her young body's contours. If her repeatedly lost shoe brings to mind her status as fairy-tale Cinderella (who had two "respectable" sisters rather than Alice's respectable half-sister), it is also "not really a slipper, but a low shoe of blue, glazed kid, rubbed and shabby,"[13] with "straps to go over the instep, but the girl only thrust her feet in" (72). The toe has a "worn point" (73), and when at the end of the story the captain puts it on her foot, he seems as a gratified a fetishist as Prince Charming. The shoe's marks of its owner, its shabbiness, worn point, and slovenly way of being worn apparently catch the captain's attention. At the story's close we learn that the captain's command was like "like a foot in the stirrup for a young man" (88), but in this story feet do not stay where they are supposed to – even when they belong to a circus-rider or her daughter.

The Planter of Malata

Sexual obsession also plays a crucial role in "The Planter of Malata." Its central male character, Geoffrey Renouard, like the young narrator-captain in "A Smile of Fortune," is a somewhat isolated individual who, away from Malata where he has started a scheme involving the experimental cultivation of silk plants, encounters the "pagan" Felicia Moorsom[14] with her "magnificently red" hair (9) and becomes fixated on her. As in "A Smile of Fortune," Conrad's male hero becomes involved in a complex game of deceptions and hidden agendas that involve not just himself and the woman by whom he has been smitten, but her father, too. The father, his sister, and his daughter have travelled from Europe to the great colonial city (Sydney in the manuscript) in search of

---

[13] The information that Alice's shoe is of kid may reflect Conrad's awareness that Cinderella's "glass slipper" has been claimed to be the result of a confusion between two French words: *vair*, a leather made from *petit-gris* (otherwise Siberian squirrel), and *verre* (glass).

[14] The name Moorsom is unusual, and Conrad may have known that Robert Moorsom captained *HMS Revenge* at the Battle of Trafalgar. "Renouard" carries with it suggestions of Reynard the fox, and in French of "reknotting," or the need to undo one's ties to begin a new life. But it cannot be said that such suggestions contribute much to the tale.

"Master Arthur," who had been engaged to Felicia but who left England in disgrace after being unjustly accused of financial wrongdoing. As Renouard knows, and as most readers guess before the fact is confirmed, "Master Arthur" is actually Renouard's assistant, Walter. And Renouard also knows that the man is dead (he buried him himself, after Walter's death following an accident), but he chooses to conceal this so as to stay in Felicia's company as long as possible. Thus, as in "A Smile of Fortune," the story presents a knot of characters each driven by publicly acknowledged as well as by secretly unacknowledged motives.

Renouard's obsession with Felicia is, like that of the narrator of "A Smile of Fortune," also presented as a sort of addiction or sickness:

> On board the schooner, lying on the settee on his back with the knuckles of his hands pressed over his eyes, he made up his mind that he would not return to that house for dinner – that he would never go back there any more. He made up his mind some twenty times. The knowledge that he had only to go up on the quarter deck, utter quietly the words: 'Man the windlass,' and that the schooner springing into life would run a hundred miles out to sea before sunrise, deceived his struggling will. Nothing easier! Yet, in the end, this young man, almost ill-famed for his ruthless daring, the inflexible leader of two tragically successful expeditions, shrank from that act of savage energy, and began, instead, to hunt for excuses. (43)

Renouard also shares with his literary predecessor the captain-narrator a consciousness of the disparity between the force of his desire and the worth of its object. However, whereas Alice Jacobus is a social outcast, Felicia belongs to "the cream of our society" (13). Her father chooses a somewhat different formulation, referring to "froth" to describe her social milieu:

> you don't know what it is to have moved, breathed, existed, and even triumphed in the mere smother and froth of life – the brilliant froth. There thoughts, sentiments, opinions, feelings, actions too, are nothing but agitation in empty space – to amuse life – a sort of superior debauchery, exciting and fatiguing, meaning nothing, leading nowhere. She is the creature of that circle. (40-41)

Conrad plays with the word "froth" to explore the treacherous combination of outer beauty and inner emptiness represented by Felicia, linking it to the foam associated with Venus's birth: "he would see her dazzling and perfect, her eyes vague, staring in mournful immobility, with a drooping head that made him think of a tragic Venus arising before him, not from the foam of the sea, but from a distant, still more formless, mysterious, and potent immensity of mankind" (36). Owen Knowles has drawn attention to the substantial debt the story owes to Mérimée's "La Vénus d'Ille" (1837), a supernatural tale in which a young man is crushed by a Roman statue of Venus to which he has been "unfaithful." (He carelessly places his ring on the statue's finger and is unable to remove it; after he marries, the statue exacts its revenge.) According to Knowles:

> The account of the statue as combining extreme beauty with the absence of sensibility finds its echo in the description of Felicia as suffering from "the insensibility of a great passion concentrated on itself" (34). Yet both she and the statue are obscurely felt to express the ultimate truth about life: the statue stands for "*la réalité*," while Felicia repeatedly announces that she stands for "truth." Such truth in physical form appears to be so witheringly final that no man can face it squarely, and both Conrad and Mérimée describe their male figures with instantly lowered eyes before the cruelly dazzling goddess-figure. (1979: 181)

Renouard's dream of the crumbling statue relies heavily on Mérimée, and, as Knowles remarks, "Like his counterpart in 'La Vénus d'Ille,' Renouard is paid a visit by a ghostly night-time version of his goddess, and feels himself crushed by the 'weight of the irremediable . . . laid on him suddenly in the small hours of the night' (23)" (1979: 182). The idea that an æsthetically powerful Roman statue stands for an absolute is easier to accept than the idea that the superficial Felicia, with her egotistic idea of self-sacrifice, does. As in "A Smile of Fortune," then, male sexual desire is seen as an intoxication inspired by a woman whose perceived unworthiness does not diminish her power to entrance. But while Alice may be presented as socially unworthy, the power of her fear and contempt to trigger feelings of sadomasochistic desire in the captain is convincingly and concretely detailed, and Conrad is able to build on this evocation of Alice's sexual allure for the captain to explain how and why his passion so suddenly evaporates.

Renouard, like the captain, also makes passionate physical contact with the object of his passion. After finally admitting to her that the missing man is dead, and declaring his own love, Renouard is similarly unable to restrain himself:

> She found herself like a feather in his grasp, helpless, unable to struggle, with her feet off the ground. But this contact with her, maddening like too much felicity, destroyed its own end. Fire ran through his veins, turned his passion to ashes, burnt him out and left him empty, without force – almost without desire. He let her go before she could cry out. (77)

If the captain's desire evaporates when Alice ceases to fear him and attempts to kiss him, this passage is curiously ambivalent about Renouard's passion and desire: the former is "turned … to ashes," while as for the latter, he is only *almost* "without desire." The ambivalence serves as a token of the story's comparative lack of focus with regard to its portrayal of male heterosexual desire. Renouard's passion turns to ashes, then, after he puts an earlier fantasy of seizing Felicia "in his arms, carrying her off in a tumult of shrieks from all these people, a silent frightened mortal, into some profound retreat as in the age of Cavern men" (45) into diminished practice. Moreover, after he has declared his passion she responds: "*Assez! J'ai horreur de tout cela*" (78), a response implying revulsion so strong as to render her incapable of expressing her horror of sex in her own language.

In perhaps less obvious ways than the earlier story, "The Planter of Malata" also explores what are now called gender roles. Owen Knowles has pointed out that since Felicia's unjustly disgraced fiancé was named Arthur, the story can be seen as "a mock-Arthurian quest" (1979: 183), with the woman in search of the man rather than vice-versa. Daphna Erdinast-Vulcan offers a convincing account of the way in which Renouard "increasingly grows to resemble [Felicia] until, at the moment when he has to make a choice between truth and lies, they are described as 'a well-matched couple, animated yet statuesque in their calmness and in their pallor'" (1999: 158). Both interpretations might be cited as evidence that Renouard has been unmanned by his passion, but such unmanning is not enacted in the convincing way that the captain's loss of the conventional attributes of masculinity is conveyed in "A Smile of Fortune." "The Planter of Malata" contains no equivalent to the darker hints about the captain's feminine side and his attraction to Alice's "masculinity" that are dropped and explored in the earlier story. Among the things that Renouard finds "ravishing" in Felicia is "the unfailing brilliance of her femininity" (35). His obsession, it is true, turns him from active adventurer to a man who goes every afternoon to Felicia's house "as passively as if in a dream" (32), but there is no sense here as in "A Smile of Fortune" that the ostensibly active hero feels a worrying pleasure in this loss of his conventional manly attributes. (The only occurrence of "manly" is its ironic and dismissive application to the "sentimental Willie," who has "manly tears" in his eyes in the opening sentence of Chapter 12.)

It is perhaps a mark of the failure of "The Planter of Malata" to grip the reader that critical accounts invariably link it with other Conrad works. *Victory*, from which Conrad was taking a break while he wrote it, is most frequently chosen for comparative comment, but *Lord Jim*, *The Secret Agent*, *Chance*, "The Return," "The Secret Sharer," and "The Informer" have all been compared to it. This list does not include "Heart of Darkness," despite the fact that, like "The Planter of Malata," it contains a "pagan" woman whose hair resembles a helmet. Felicia's "ivory forehead" (35) also carries echoes of Conrad's best-known work. In terms of her *inner* qualities Felicia has more in common with Kurtz's Intended than his African mistress: she exhibits utter and self-sacrificing faithfulness to an unworthy man, even after his death. Like Alice, then, though in very different ways, she combines some of the characteristics of these two figures. Another possible cross-reference is suggested reluctantly. Felicia's sudden recourse to French, which Alice speaks on several occasions, may remind us of Natalia Haldin of *Under Western Eyes*. But there are more telling structural parallels between these two works to which it is worth devoting some attention.

At the heart of both "The Planter of Malata" and *Under Western Eyes* is a pattern of non-symmetrical lines of attraction that can be summarized as follows. Man A has had some knowledge of and/or involvement in Man B's death. Man A meets and falls in love with a woman who has close ties with Man B, but Man A does not at first reveal the extent (or, in the case of "The Planter of Malata," the fact) of his relationship with Man B. When he does so, the woman recoils in horror, and the man sacrifices himself, literally or metaphorically. (If this sacrifice is as much reminiscent of Victor Haldin as it is of Razumov, one might note that Renouard's posture at the opening of Chapter 6 – "lying on the settee on his back with the knuckles of his hands pressed over his eyes" [43] – also recalls Natalia Haldin's brother.)

Under Western Eyes is vastly superior to "The Planter of Malata," but this repeated pattern suggests that Conrad saw unavowed knowledge as a form of power that corrupted a personal relationship. Razumov, too, gains perverted pleasure from the power of his secret knowledge of Victor Haldin's death when in the presence of his sister. One of the best critics of "The Planter of Malata," Joel R Kehler, has argued that in the novella Conrad attempted "a sort of mini-epic in twelve sections of the nature, limits, and consequences of knowledge" (1976: 149). This is well-put, and certainly takes in those claims to total knowledge made by journalists and the press, a subsidiary theme in "The Planter of Malata," as much as the corrupting effect of unavowed knowledge in personal relations. However, one of the reasons why Conrad's earlier novel provides so much deeper and sophisticated an analysis of male sexual desire than does "The Planter of Malata" is that in *Under Western Eyes* Conrad is able to look at desire as manifested in two very different characters: Razumov and the older teacher of languages. An additional and more telling reason is that Natalia is a far more substantial character (in terms of literary portrayal and depicted human terms) than Alice or, especially, Felicia. One basic inadequacy in "The Planter of Malata" – set in sharper relief if one reads it alongside "A Smile of Fortune" – is that because Felicia is so trivial, the claim that Renouard is attracted to her personality is unbelievable. While what attracts the captain to Alice is comprehensively and concretely detailed, the power Felicia asserts over Renouard is merely asserted.

In both works Conrad is concerned to investigate the extent to which personality can be expressed physically, in the body and its behaviour. After Renouard's meeting with the Editor at the opening of "The Planter of Malata," for example, we read: "Because of the force of the physical impression he had received from her personality (and such impressions are the real origins of the deepest movements of our soul) this conception [i.e., as "subjugated by something common"] of her was even inconceivable" (22). In the manuscript of *Under Western Eyes* deletions and amendments to a sequence in which the teacher of languages attempts to explain his attraction to Natalia display this same concern to explore the interaction between the physical and the personality:

> She directed upon me her grey eyes shaded by black eyelashes and I became aware [how attractive her personality was] notwithstanding my years how attractive physically her personality [was] could be to a man [looking for] capable of appreciating something else in a woman than the mere grace of femininity.
> (2003: 293; words enclosed in square brackets deleted in MS)

Conrad's manuscript amendments show how hard he worked to adjust his words to his perception that Natalia's human profundity involves an intermingling of an attractive and complex personality and a desirable body. I use the word "intermingling" because Conrad seems concerned to stress that Natalia's personality finds – among other things – *bodily* expression. But there is nothing in the presentation of Felicia to suggest that her personality has anything of the depth or complexity of Natalia's. Indeed, the contrast between the presentation of the captain's perception of Alice Jacobus's desirability and the presentation of Renouard's cataclysmically passionate enslavement by Felicia could hardly be greater. Assertions in the generalized language of melodrama replace telling concrete detail:

> her hair was magnificently red and her eyes very black. It was a troubling effect, but it had been evanescent.... The light from an open window fell across her path, and suddenly all that mass of arranged hair appeared incandescent, chiselled and fluid, with the daring suggestion of a helmet of burnished copper and the flowing lines of molten metal. It kindled in him an astonished admiration. (9-10)

It is not just that Felicia's "magnificently red" and "arranged" hair comes off badly when set against Alice's "dishevelled magnificent hair of a gipsy tramp." Certainly, when Renouard gazes at the tip of Felicia's shoe (36), the footwear has none of the erotic charge that Alice's slipper gathers. Most important, though, is that the initial insistence on concreteness (the passage begins by focussing attention on the physical) moves anti-climactically to an assertion couched in adjectival insistence and banal generality. Towards the story's end, this gets even worse. Felicia's bemusement at Renouard's suggestion that she is an aristocrat prompts him (or Conrad) into yet more embarrassing excess:

> "you are merely of the topmost layer, disdainful and superior, the mere pure froth and bubble on the inscrutable depths which some day will toss you out of existence. But you are you! You are you! You are the eternal love itself – only, O Divinity, it isn't your body, it is your soul that is made of foam." (76-77)

The reader can be forgiven for wondering what is happening here.

Daphna Erdinast-Vulcan has described such passages as "pseudo-poetic discourse, an indiscriminate outpouring of lovers' sentimentality, crude enough to sound like a parody of itself." She notes, too, that "the narrative throughout the story does not dissociate itself from the discourse of the protagonist" (1999: 163). Beyond its sentimentality, Renouard's "outpouring" is contradictory: how can he admit that Felicia is "the mere pure froth and bubble" with "a soul that is made of foam," while acclaiming her as "eternal love itself" and as a "Divinity"? The passage combines unambiguous insult with an outpouring of unbounded love. What woman could respond positively to such a declaration? Notably, "The Planter of Malata," apart from the occasional sarcasm, lacks humour. "A Smile of Fortune," in contrast, is possessed of a vein of droll and self-deprecatory mockery that may well have served to shield against melodrama: wholehearted indulgence in the melodramatic cannot long survive humour or irony.

Conrad's late memoir "Stephen Crane" attributes the original idea for "The Planter of Malata" to Crane. The essay recalls an evening during which Crane told him of "a subject for a story … He called it 'The Predecessor.'" Crane wanted Conrad to collaborate with him in turning the idea into a play, but the collaboration never took place: "The general subject consisted in a man personating his 'predecessor' (who had died) in the hope of winning a girl's heart … and the action, I fear, would have been frankly melodramatic" (*Last Essays*, 115). One wonders to what extent Conrad is here half-consciously attempting to shift blame on to Crane for the melodramatic elements in "The Planter of Malata."

If "A Smile of Fortune" casts Alice as Cinderella and the captain as a Prince Charming *manqué*, "The Planter of Malata" seems unsure with which fairy tale it wishes to associate itself.[15] In Chapter 3, Renouard dismisses the idea that the missing Master Arthur might be worthy of Felicia: "But no Prince Charming has ever lived out of a fairy tale. He doesn't walk the worlds of Fashion and Finance – and with a stumbling gait at that" (22). Professor Moorsom, though, on learning that Arthur is not on Malata, comments: "How vexingly elusive the poor fellow has become! I'll begin to think that some wicked fairy is favouring this love tale with unpleasant attentions" (64).

The novella, however, contains a dark, indirect reference to Perrault's "Blue Beard." After upsetting Renouard with his suggestion that they investigate the belief in ghosts among the plantation "boys," Felicia's father attempts to placate him: "We are all of us a little strung up," he said. "For my part I have been like sister Anne in the story. But I cannot see anything coming. Anything that would be the least good for anybody – I mean" (70). In Perrault's tale, Sister Anne waits at the window looking out for the arrival of the two brothers who will save the heroine from Blue Beard, who is calling for her to come to him. Eventually, the brothers burst in, just preventing Blue Beard from adding the heroine's body to those of his other murdered wives. Blue Beard is killed, and the heroine marries "a very worthy man, who banished from her mind all memory of the evil days she had spent with Blue Beard." If Professor Moorsom is Sister Anne, he must be hinting that Master

---

[15] Both works are packed with intertextual allusions. Watts (1985) mentions a number in "A Smile of Fortune," including "The Sleeping Beauty," which also boasts an imprisoned heroine in a walled garden. Erdinast-Vulcan (1999) draws a parallel to the plot of *The Tempest* (although with a different outcome) and relates Alfred Jacobus to the biblical Jacob, who impersonates his brother Esau. Kirschner (1966) and Hervouet (1990) have traced Conrad's heavy reliance on Maupassant's "Les Sœurs Rondoli" (1884) for the portrayal of the alluring Alice, and they as well as Knowles (1979) have shown how Anatole France, Maupassant, and Mérimée have, as Hervouet puts it, left "tangible marks" on "The Planter of Malata." If phrases and short sequences in "A Smile of Fortune" seem directly from "Les Sœurs Rondoli," "The Planter of Malata" owes a comparable debt to Mérimée's "La Vénus d'Ille" (1837), but this similarity is also a difference: the allusions and intertextual links in "A Smile of Fortune" combine to achieve a subtextual symphonic force, but in "The Planter of Malata" the associations produce discord rather than harmony.

Arthur is Blue Beard, and perhaps, too, that Renouard might be the "very worthy man" who will banish from his daughter's mind the evil days spent with and in pursuit of Arthur. But Arthur is a poor Blue Beard and can be assigned the role only in his threat to destroy the life of the woman searching for him. Moreover, Renouard will not marry Felicia. Thus, if "A Smile of Fortune" is an anti-Cinderella, "The Planter of Malata" is an anti-Blue Beard.

Even though when he first meets her Renouard detects something "pagan" (9) in Felicia's appearance, the attribution is unjustified by anything revealed about her. Indeed, the association seems at odds with the repeated insistence on her membership of a mindless, upper-class set. Conrad may perhaps be attempting to provide a basis for his classical allusions – the references to Minerva, Pallas Athena, and Mérimée's statue – but the reader sees nothing pagan about Miss Moorsom. Indeed, the difference in class between her and Alice Jacobus may have much to do with the fact that although both female characters are the cause and object of sexual obsession, Alice's appearances in "A Smile of Fortune" invariably crackle with an erotic charge while Felicia is as erotic as one of Renouard's bales of vegetable silks. Conrad's sense of the erotic does not seem capable of depicting convincingly the attraction that active men feel for upper-class, "society" women. (Lingard's romantic involvement with Mrs. Travers in *The Rescue* offers another example of such an unconvincing depiction.)

The weakness of "The Planter of Malata" is perhaps most apparent in its dialogue, and appropriately it opens with a conversation between Renouard and a newspaper proprietor-editor, a scene in which chunks of story are filled in by an omniscient narrator's explanatory comment. Such omniscience always risks undermining a sense of dramatic event and potentiality, and in this scene the characters are puppet-like compared to those of "A Smile of Fortune," who are generally observed in dramatic situations from the involved participant's point-of-view. In his "Author's Note" to *Within the Tides*, in which "The Planter of Malata" was published in book form, Conrad claims that the collection's three stories were "written at different times, under various influences, and with the deliberate intention of trying several ways of telling a tale" (ix). Whether or not this is to be believed, the story's narrative technique has a sense of artificiality when contrasted to the flow and natural ease of "A Smile of Fortune." Were "The Planter of

Malata" a first-person narrative told from Renouard's perspective some of its worst melodramatic excesses might well have been avoided.

Daphna Erdinast-Vulcan argues that "the genre of romance, which Conrad had apparently relegated to the realm of women, unleashed the writer's own pathological fear of losing his 'masculine' self and his deeply rooted misogyny, which is nowhere more conspicuous than when he sets out to 'write for women'" (1999: 170). As far as "The Planter of Malata" is concerned this is plausible; as Erdinast-Vulcan notes, the face that Renouard sees in the mirror is not that of the "'true Renouard' because, in his desire to replace the missing lover, he has exchanged his old self for the dead man, the creature of [Felicia's] romantic discourse" (1999: 159). "A Smile of Fortune" is another matter. Although the *captain* may indeed be afraid of losing his conventionally masculine self, Conrad displays no æsthetic fear of this topic, no unwillingness to explore the fact that a considerable part of the erotic excitement that Alice stirs in the captain can be enjoyed by him only when, taking advantage of the opportunities offered by the liminal space of the harbour, he escapes from his respectable masculine self into opposed but linked erotic experiences in which he enjoys the drugged pleasure generated by Alice's fear and contempt. In "The Planter of Malata," Renouard finds "ravishing" Felicia's "quietness" and "the unfailing brilliance of her femininity" (35), things unlikely to challenge conventional gender roles.

Is "A Smile of Fortune" better than "The Planter of Malata" because it recognizes that elements of sadism and masochism are integral to male sexual desire while the latter doesn't? In part, yes. Only "in part" because I do not believe that sexuality leads a peaceful existence untouched by history and culture. Sexualization is always deeply implicated in issues of class, race, power, and culture, and the Ripper and Dr Crippen cases – their occurrence and sensationalized depiction in the press – must be seen as extreme manifestations of the fact that significant veins of power and violence ran through male eroticism at the time Conrad was writing and about which he was writing. His awareness of these cases while composing "A Smile of Fortune" may well have helped him trace significant veins of power and violence in his experience of the erotic and in his depiction of it.

In both these historical periods, European male sexuality had its public, acknowledged, face and its secret, unacknowledged one. In a world in which men "enjoyed" (in both senses of the word) legal and social power over women, such enjoyment entered into forming sexual identity and patterns of arousal. "A Smile of Fortune" confronts the residue of social and gender inequality in contemporary male sexuality by exploring the captain-narrator's contradictorily sadistic and masochistic desire for Alice in the (appropriately) no-man's land of the harbour. He eats of the fruit of knowledge springing from the roots of his sexual desire and reaches the honest and damning conclusion that his desire leaves a smell of corruption.

Whatever lies behind or constitutes Conrad's "decline" in the years following his completion of *Under Western Eyes* – if one accepts that such a decline occurred – the evidence of these novellas suggests that it is not a concern to depict and explore sexuality and the erotic. At the heart of the disturbing power of "A Smile of Fortune" is precisely the evocation of and investigation into the sources of heterosexual erotic desire and experience, while the inert and lifeless quality of "The Planter of Malata" cannot be separated from its laying claim to erotic experience on the part of Renouard that it is unable to present in a convincingly enacted form because its social and cultural roots remain untraced.

Acknowledgements

My thanks are due to Paul Goring, who obtained useful material for me, and to Stephen Donovan, whose comments on a draft of this essay have been invaluable.

Works cited

Bagnall, Peter. *Joseph Conrad and Jack the Ripper.* Ph.D. diss., University of Oxford, 1999.

Baines, Jocelyn. *Joseph Conrad: A Critical Biography.* 1960; rpt. London: Penguin, 1971.

Billy, Ted. *A Wilderness of Words: Closure and Disclosure in Conrad's Short Fiction.* Lubbock: Texas Tech University Press, 1997.

Conrad, Joseph. *Collected Edition of the Works of Joseph Conrad.* 22 vols. London: J. M. Dent & Sons, 1946-1955

———. *Under Western Eyes.* Edited by Jeremy Hawthorn. Oxford: Oxford University Press, 2003.

Elbert, Monika. "The Ligeia Syndrome, or, Many 'Happy Returns,' in Conrad's Gothic." *Conradiana* 33 (Summer 2001): 129-52.

Erdinast-Vulcan, Daphna. *The Strange Short Fiction of Joseph Conrad: Writing, Culture, and Subjectivity.* Oxford: Oxford University Press, 1999.

Graver, Lawrence. *Conrad's Short Fiction.* Berkeley and Los Angeles: University of California Press, 1969.

Hampson, Robert. "Silence and Secrets in Joseph Conrad's *Victory.*" *Chia Journal of Humanities and Social Sciences* 3 (November 2001): 225-46.

Hervouet, Yves. *The French Face of Joseph Conrad.* Cambridge: Cambridge University Press, 1990.

Jones, Susan. *Conrad and Women.* Oxford: Clarendon Press, 1999.

Kehler, Joel R. "'The Planter of Malata': Renouard's Sinking Star of Knowledge." *Conradiana* 8 (1976): 148-62.

Kirschner, Paul. "Conrad and Maupassant: Moral Solitude and 'A Smile of Fortune.'" *Review of English Literature* 7 (1966): 62-77.

Knowles, Owen. "Conrad and Mérimée: The Legend of Venus in 'The Planter of Malata.'" *Conradiana* 11 (1979): 177-84.

———, and Gene M. Moore. *Oxford Reader's Companion to Conrad.* Oxford: Oxford University Press, 2000.

Moser, Thomas C. *Joseph Conrad: Achievement and Decline.* Cambridge, Mass.: Harvard University Press, 1957.

Najder, Zdzisław. *Joseph Conrad: A Chronicle.* Cambridge: Cambridge University Press, 1983.

Ray, Martin, ed. *Joseph Conrad: Interviews and Recollections.* London: Macmillan, 1990.

Roberts, Andrew Michael, *Conrad and Masculinity.* Houndmills: Macmillan Press, 2000.

———, ed. *Conrad and Gender.* Amsterdam – Atlanta: Rodopi, 1993.

Said, Edward W. *Joseph Conrad and the Fiction of Autobiography.* Cambridge, Mass.: Harvard University Press, 1966.

Thorburn, David. *Conrad's Romanticism.* New Haven: Yale University Press, 1974.

Watts, Cedric. "The Narrative Enigma of Conrad's 'A Smile of Fortune.'" *Conradiana* 17 (1985): 131-36.

Zuckerman, Jerome. "'A Smile of Fortune': Conrad's Interesting Failure." *Studies in Short Fiction* 2 (1964): 99-102.

"Petticoats" and "Sea Business": Women Characters in Conrad's Edwardian Short Stories

Jennifer Turner
University of Hull

IN 1912, CONRAD WROTE to Edward Garnett describing "The Secret Sharer" with rare enthusiasm: "No damned tricks with girls there. Eh? Every word fits and there's not a single uncertain note" (*CL*5: 128). The flippant tone encourages the stereotype of Conrad as a misogynistic writer of sea stories for and about men, a characterization he objected to: "This damned sea business keeps off as many people as it gathers in."[1] Yet the sea features in all of Conrad's novels, even if indirectly – Winnie Verloc's leap into the English Channel in *The Secret Agent* (1907) – or only briefly – Peter Ivanovitch's escape from Russia in *Under Western Eyes* (1911). Nonetheless, Conrad's annoyance at being categorized as a "sea-writer" suggests that whatever the pervasive presence of the sea in his work, he did not consider it his central conceit. With respect to his female characters the emphasis is reversed: despite the complaint that women characters figure infrequently in Conrad's writing, "The Secret Sharer" is his only story not to introduce one. Attributing the tale's artistic success to its exclusively male concerns, Conrad did, however, admit "tricks with girls" in his other stories even asking Garnett: "Do you think one can make something interesting without any women?!" (*CL*1: 171). The question implies that however reluctant Conrad was to write about women, he had to do so not merely for the sake of popularity but out of interest. His description of "The Secret Sharer" is a deliberate attempt to deflect and confuse or an admission that women represent one of his most problematic concerns.

---

[1] Letter to Richard Curle, 17 July 1923; Jean-Aubry 1927, 2:321.

Conrad criticism has traditionally considered the women characters of the sea stories as unnecessary, unsubstantial, and artless concessions to public taste. This issue, however, seems to have polarized criticism from the start. One reviewer commended *The Nigger of the "Narcissus"* (1897) because "There is not a petticoat in all Mr Conrad's pages" (Knowles and Moore 2000: 126); on the other hand, the *Daily Mail*'s reviewer lamented that "the only female in the book is the ship herself" (cited in Jones 1999: 11). Some critics even admire Conrad's sea tales *because* of the relative marginalization of women characters, considering it a noble artistic refusal to submit to popular pressures. Yet they tend to ignore that in writing about the sea Conrad was actively seeking commercial success. Ironically, although women and the sea belong to the same "popular" literary category, the latter subject is generally thought the more "artistic," with writing about women condemned to the separate, lesser genre of "romance." For Conrad, however, the "potboiler," a format evoking few expectations of originality or depth, seems to have allowed greater freedom for experimentation, as his manipulation of the genre creates a sense of awkwardness in the "serious" reader that reflects the awkwardness of the subject matter. Little has been written about the possible connections between "petticoats" and "sea business," particularly in "Freya of the Seven Isles" (1912) and "A Smile of Fortune" (1912), in which Conrad seems to play with, and subvert the conventions of "popular" literature by using women characters and the qualities they represent to dominate the action.

The women characters in Conrad's stories are generally more powerful, glamorous, and erotic than their counterparts in the novels, holding an explicit physical power over men. In "Freya of the Seven Isles," the narrator describes the heroine as "the kind of a girl one remembers … She could – Jasper told me once with a touchingly imbecile exultation – sit on her hair" (149-50). For Conrad, the short story and perhaps the disguise of a "sea" tale might have represented a flirtatious deviation, allowing a temporary release of repressed voyeuristic impulse and the consequent development of a new kind of heroine. Yet, as in the novels, male relationships with women rarely succeed, and many are tarnished by money, as is that between Alice and the narrator of "A Smile of Fortune." The latter feels pressured to accept Alice's father, Jacobus, as ship's chandler and honour-bound to buy a shipment of potatoes. Similarly, the eponymous Freya refuses to marry Jasper before he makes his fortune. Women and money seem to represent the two main contaminating shore influences, severing the bond between sailor and sea and destabilizing a traditional masculinist mythology of toil and reward. Such disruption might also represent Conrad's displaced sense of himself as an artist, feeling his integrity compromised by desire and financial need and finding metaphors for the tensions of his writing career in his prior maritime experience. His sea stories seem obsessed with such dangerous influences, and he was apparently drawn to *femmes fatales*, even sardonically and perhaps self-critically enjoying imperiling his male characters.

This essay will investigate Conrad's own precarious investment in an idealistic sea mythology in his early writing before focusing on the least traditional of his sea stories, the tales in which women are given as much dominance as the sea and whose very titles announce their place in popular fiction: "Falk" (1903), "The Brute" (1908), "A Smile of Fortune," and "Freya of the Seven Isles." In these Edwardian stories the narrator is anonymous, a figure limited to his individual tale, once again suggesting a brief flirtation that Conrad wished, perhaps guiltily, to keep separate.

I

The 7th-century Anglo-Saxon poem "The Seafarer" captures a heroic spirit of endurance and strength in adversity, evoking a primordial connection between man and the elements. Moreover, it provides a traditional mythology (in the sense of a popular and collective, as opposed to a purely fictitious notion) of the volatile sea and undaunted seafarer, a comparison particularly suitable for Conrad, whose fictional and autobiographical maritime writing explores the similar tensions between tortuous hardship and indefatigable devotion. Yet in his late essay "Legends," posthumously published in *Last Essays* in 1926, Conrad sceptically describes such mythologies – the "imaginative recognition of the past" (44) – as "disfigured by touches of fatuity of which no legend is wholly free, because I suspect that those who record its tales as picked out on the lips of men are doing it in a spirit of love" (44). Nostalgia and bias taint memory, but such "fatuity" also paradoxically affirms love. As Conrad finally concedes: "The facts of a legend need not be literally true.

But they ought to be credible and they must be in a sort of fundamental accord with the nature of the life they record" (46). Since "love is uncritical" (44), however, there is a genuine danger of the subjective overwhelming the objective, thereby creating a misleading mythology that, if adopted as a model to live by, invariably leads to disillusion. In his sea stories, then, Conrad tempers nostalgia with self-awareness, emphasizing the contrast between early idealism and painful reality.

His heightened awareness of this contrast is demonstrated in the fictionalizing of his own voyage in the ill-fated *Palestine* in 1881-82 in "Youth" (1898). The narrator's description of Marlow's tale as a "chronicle" (3), combined with the all-male company and the age-old practice of storytelling itself, evokes a parallel with Viking or, even, as the mahogany table suggests, Arthurian legend. Yet the dual narrative, as the older Marlow recounts the words and deeds of his younger self with mixed irony and regret – while also contributing his own more pessimistic interpretation of events – undermines the notion of a single, stable "mythology." The young Marlow lives by his ship's motto "Do or Die" (12), refusing to allow three near-disasters to dampen his enthusiasm for his journey eastwards or his new position as second mate. The young Marlow's over-investment in traditional mythologies of, for example, the voyage as a rite of passage, the East as an exotic adventure, and youth as an unlimited privilege, seems to have made him unfit for the sea in later life. His disillusion and sorrow are so great as to be debilitating. A narrative that wavers between hyperbole, mock-heroic irony, and regret undermines enthusiasm and idealism.

The older, more experienced Marlow, a jaded, introspective figure, constantly stresses the disjunction between past and present: "O youth! The strength of it, the faith of it, the imagination of it! To me she [the *Judea*] was not an old rattle-trap carting about the world a lot of coal for a freight – to me she was the endeavour, the test, the trial of life" (12). The older Marlow feels alienated from the carefree and fearless mythologies of youth. From his overarching perspective, courage and dedication no longer necessarily lead to victory or reward: "there are those voyages that seem ordered for the illustration of life, that might stand for a symbol of existence. You fight, work, sweat, nearly kill yourself, sometimes do kill yourself, trying to accomplish something – and you can't" (3-4).

Conrad's gendering of the sea highlights the corrosion of a traditional male mythology. Although in the manuscript of "The Heart of Darkness" it is referred to as a "master," in the printed version it is a "mistress" (48), a time-honoured feminization Conrad uses repeatedly. The term suggests a sense of personal subordination and a long-standing love affair, two meanings equally pervasive in Conrad's writings. The idea of the sea as a powerful and seductive female lover is recurrent, as for example in the "Author's Note" to *The Mirror of the Sea*, where Conrad describes his relationship with the sea as a great "love story" (x) that "went on unreasoning and invincible, surviving the test of disillusion, defying the disenchantment that lurks in every day of a strenuous life; went on full of love's delight and love's anguish … without bitterness and without repining, from the first hour to the last" (ix-x). However, this idealized bond is prone to waver, with Conrad revealing distinct signs of "bitterness":

> the ocean has no compassion, no faith, no law, no memory. Its fickleness is to be held true to men's purposes only by an undaunted resolution and by a sleepless, armed, jealous vigilance, in which, perhaps, there has always been more hate than love. (135)

The "love story" is a tempestuous one since the powerful and potentially dangerous "mistress" requires constant and exclusive attention. Moreover, the sea's feminine nature seems to extend to the ships sailing upon her, with Conrad prescribing a similar blend of devotion and caution: "your ship wants to be humoured with knowledge. You must treat with an understanding consideration the mysteries of her feminine nature, and then she will stand by you faithfully in the unceasing struggle with forces wherein defeat is no shame" (56). *The Mirror of the Sea* even seems to be a kind of marital guidebook, documenting the various female personalities of different ships and warning against negligence. Indeed, a fear of angering either the sea or, apparently by extension, the ship, recurs throughout Conrad's writings, creating the discomforting notion of a love/hate relationship with a jealous, potentially vengeful lover.

Conrad seems actively to have avoided commitments at sea, changing ship comparatively often (serving on at least eleven vessels over a twenty-year period), a restlessness that suggests impulsiveness, fickleness, or a fear of becoming overly attached. After marrying in 1896, he effectively retired as a sailor. Moreover, his writing constantly stresses the incompatibility of married life with life at sea. In "Youth," Captain Beard, having briefly abandoned his ship to protect his wife, warns Marlow against making family ties: "A sailor has no business with a wife – I say. There I was, out of the ship. Well, no harm done this time" (9). In *Chance* (1913), Conrad's longest study of the disruptive influence of a woman aboard ship, Anthony's marriage generates a flood of paranoia and resentment amongst his crew, particularly in the first mate Franklin, who reminisces to Powell: "you haven't known the ship as she used to be. She was more than a home to a man. She was not like any other ship; and Captain Anthony was not like any other master to sail with. Neither is she now. But before one never had a care in the world as to her – and as to him, too" (287).

Franklin even seems afraid of the disruption in the relationship between man and ship. The sea, it seems, does not tolerate a rival. (Anthony finally goes down with his ship.) Conrad's infamous seasickness in the Channel during his wedding night might, then, be interpreted as evidence of fear or guilt for having betrayed his first love, yet his preoccupation with the sea also suggests a continuing infatuation even after his marriage, an almost morbid fascination with a mistress he was by then both in awe and afraid of. Ultimately, the sailor and the writer found themselves allied to very different females.

II

In his Edwardian stories Conrad seems preoccupied with the question of and possible solution to divided loyalties. In "Falk" he addresses the potential clash between man and sea, exploring the definition and safe limits of masculinity. The male name of Falk's first ship honours its builder, *Borgmester Dahl.* The ship is considered a great achievement, the pride of her hometown, yet once at sea she soon deteriorates, fulfilling the narrator's ominous warning: "A misunderstanding between a man and his ship … is bound to end in trouble for the man" (189). The loss of the rudder suggests castration, or a reassertion of female power, that leaves the crew emasculated; her drifting into Arctic waters, combined with the crew's isolation, echoes the situation in "The Ancient Mariner." The cannibalism that ensues seems, moreover, to represent a series of metaphorical rapes, with Falk becoming the dominant predator. Significantly, Conrad re-uses this trope as the captain-narrator describes Falk's towing of Hermann's ship: "I could not have believed that a simple towing operation could suggest so plainly the idea of abduction, of rape" (170). As suggested by his name, Falk has been dehumanized by his actions, regressing to a mere creature of instinct: "He wanted to live. He had always wanted to live. So we all do – but in us the instinct serves a complex conception, and in him this instinct existed alone" (223). The word "alone" emphasizes his ostracism and social isolation as the *Borgmester Dahl*'s male community destroys itself.

Though the narrator proves himself a helpful mediator, the only character apparently capable of helping Falk is Hermann's silent niece, precisely because she has the same physical qualities as his previous ship: "she was built on a magnificent scale. Built is the only word. She was constructed, she was erected, as it were, with regal lavishness" (151). The absence of her name and voice emphasizes her statuesque appearance and mythological associations; her constant sewing, for example, evokes the Fates. Her silence seems to make her a mere figurehead of romance, contrasting with Falk's desperate desire to speak and confess, again suggesting female power over an unstable male mythology. She even seems to represent an antidote to Falk's death instinct, the embodiment of the life force: "she could have stood for an allegoric statue of the Earth. I don't mean the worn-out earth of our possession, but a young Earth, a virginal planet undisturbed by the vision of a future teeming with the monstrous forms of life, clamorous with the cruel battles of hunger and thought" (152).

Hermann's ship, the *Diana*, with its association with the Roman goddess of the hunt, suggests a significant parallel with Falk. The niece represents another instinctual being, but conversely, one of sympathy and feeling as Conrad evokes the stereotypical primal natures of male and female. Female influences in this story, therefore, are capable of both destroying and reconstructing the male psyche, not through words but through their mere presence, undermining the illusion of control and forcing an admission of weakness. Only another female, it seems, can reverse the effects of the female sea/ship, and the male narrator consequently remains uneasy with Falk's new alliance. His final glimpse of the couple reveals Falk in a pose of submission and dependence:

> He held her hands and looked down at them, and she looked up at him with her candid and unseeing glance. It seemed to me they had come together as if attracted, drawn and guided to each other by a mysterious influence. They were a complete couple. In her gray frock, palpitating with life, generous of form, olympian and simple, she was indeed the siren to fascinate that dark navigator, this ruthless lover of the five senses. (239)

If the sea is a ruthless siren, Hermann's niece is merely a different kind. A seemingly romantic resolution is undercut by a discomforting sense of the primal as Falk is less cured than controlled and spellbound.

"The Brute" (1908) further sensationalizes the emotions of paranoia and fear in "Falk." The opening page seems specifically designed to shock as an anonymous voice declares: "That fellow Wilmot fairly dashed her brains out, and a good job, too!" (105). This defiant triumphalism suggests grim satisfaction in the destruction of "her," whom we later discover to be a ship that, as the unidentified internal narrator reveals, resists, often violently, all attempts at control: "There are ships difficult to handle, but generally you can depend on them behaving rationally. With *that* ship, whatever you did with her you never knew how it would end. She was a wicked beast. Or, perhaps, she was only just insane" (111-12). Whereas the *Borgmester Dahl* is only passively malevolent, *The Apse Family* is actively so. Whether mad or inherently malicious, the ship is consistently female, and her often-fatal attacks on the men around her are presented as vitriolic and vindictive (by implication qualities particularly feminine). She is compared to "a big hearse" (115) as her reputation for murder grows, evoking an uncanny sense of superstition and dread.

As in "Falk," an assertion of female power threatens male identity. By contrast with the ship in "Falk," however, the temperamental "Brute" seems to attract men. The relationship between man and ship in the story is disturbing and even morbid. To serve and survive in the brute-ship represents manhood's ultimate test, one the narrator is drawn to despite his protests. His supposed reason for joining the crew – a reluctance to offend the ship's owners – hardly seems reasonable in the face of his father's natural disinclination against having two sons in the same ship. In fact, the narrator's professed hatred for the "brute" seems part of a male conspiracy intended to deceive and mislead the reader into accepting their "myth" of events. Even the aforementioned introduction appears contrived to destabilize the reader's sense of judgement in an attempt to regain control. As the story subsequently attempts to justify its controversial opening, the narrative actively seeks to challenge moral preconceptions, a daunting task that inclines the reader merely to accept the male version as established by the four men in the parlour. This story has often, then, been interpreted as another example of Conrad's alleged misogyny though it was published two years after *The Mirror of the Sea*, in which Conrad proclaimed that "No ship is wholly bad … there can be no harm in affirming that in these vanished generations of willing servants there never has been one utterly unredeemable soul" (119-20).

The most obvious inconsistency in the persistent feminization of "the brute" is that the ship's name is gender neutral, encompassing both male and female members of the Apse family. The name's inclusiveness even suggests that it is the clash and conflict between the sexes has created the monster. Moreover, the only other ship referred to in the story, the *Lucy Apse*, is portrayed as idyllic by comparison, implying that it may be less the brute's feminine side that is to blame than the male, as reinforced by the masculine connotations of the word "brute." The company's desire to build a superior vessel, using only the finest materials, evokes "heroic" notions of ambition and power, but also implies a dangerous arrogance, with Conrad condemning a male attempt at control. *The Apse Family* built, like the *Borgmester Dahl*, to represent the company's power and wealth, seems invested with too much male mythology, disrupting the precarious relationship between the ship and her crew and thereby creating an internal rebellion. The brute herself thus becomes a victim, a misunderstood freak, constructed yet disavowed by man.

An emphasis on senseless and tragic events also seems designed to manipulate the reader's prejudice against the brute. Maggie's drowning, as a loose anchor drags her into the sea, is presented as an avenging mistress's jealous attack. Yet, ironically, in *The Mirror of the Sea*, Conrad not only refers to the anchor as "a symbol of hope" (15), a traditional association, but links it to the first mate, the actual position of Maggie's *fiancé* Charley, whose failure to understand the nature of *The Apse Family* and to protect Maggie from that ship makes him as much to blame as the ship itself. Moreover, their marriage is hinted at only obliquely, suggesting an attempt to obscure this relationship and outwit the ship, foolishly tempting fate, as does the narrator with his premature and misguided cry: "You've tamed her" (122). The brute subsequently undermines the illusion of control as the men onboard prove unable to protect the women, as the pilot's crazed words emphasize: "Killing women, now! Killing women, now!" (124). The horrific description of Maggie's death and Charley's despair seem designed to obscure male mistakes. The brute becomes a scapegoat as male culpability is disguised in attacks on female nature.

The male narrator initially attributes the ship's final destruction to the nightwatchman Wilmot, but the narrative stresses the "green-eyed governess, or nurse" (127) with whom Wilmot is infatuated. (The description "green-eyed" reinforces jealousy as the story's dominant emotion.) The actual wrecking, moreover, is depicted as an attempted murder gone wrong, though in reality it is caused by Wilmot's negligence.

The ship and governess seem inextricably linked as the narrator describes their parallel fates, the one crashing against the shore as the other is knocked under the table. The condemnation, "deserved nothing better," also implies a misogynistic idea of ignominy at having been finally destroyed by a woman. The narrator cannot relinquish his hatred of the ship and, by extension, of women. Ironically, however, these attacks on the brute as a female entity ultimately mean that, as in "Falk," female mythology is able to claim the story's combined physical and supernatural power, eclipsing the male. The governess finally puts an end to the destructive cycle as, once again, female overcomes female. Moreover, another and frequently overlooked, woman in the story, Miss Blank, the barmaid of The Three Crows, an impassive figure who in opening and closing the narrative frames the whole of it with a female influence. She is also the only woman who speaks, although outside the internal narrator's story. Her name, however, seems to represent a sly joke, emphasizing how identity can be imposed, often unfairly and ill advisedly, from without.

III

In 1908, Conrad received a visit from a Captain Carlos M. Marris, an admirer from the East, who urged him to return to his literary roots with more Eastern sea tales. It seems possible that after his breakdown in 1911, and the commercial failure of *The Secret Agent* and *Under Western Eyes*, Conrad may also felt the need for a change, as well as being inspired by the idea of a lucrative waiting audience. The stories of this period differ distinctly from their predecessors, the main change being the increased importance of women characters, a change often regarded as a commercial sell-out and a factor contributing to Moser's achievement-and-decline theory.

In "A Smile of Fortune," the narrator is also the main character, a rare occurrence as Conrad generally chose a more distanced narrative voice. The captain-narrator's personal involvement suggests an autobiographical context, and several critics have noted the likely connections between the story's sultry Alice Jacobus, Eugénie Renouf, the French woman who encouraged and spurned Conrad on Mauritius in 1888, and Alice Shaw, the real-life shipping agent's 17-year-old daughter on that same island. Moreover, the change in the narrator's perception of the island, as it develops from a "pearl" into a place he is eager to escape from, seems to echo Conrad's disillusionment. Ironically, he seems to derive masochistic enjoyment out of reliving his own unhappy experiences in this viciously ironic black comedy, variously suggesting a cathartic need to admit his mistakes, a desire to rebuild his damaged relationship with the sea, or, less laudably, an act of revenge on the women who, he felt, betrayed him.

"A Smile of Fortune" is a tale of self-betrayal and degradation as the confident captain-narrator, despite repeated warnings, is lured into the company of Alice, the petulant, ungracious daughter of the mysterious ship's chandler Jacobus. His resulting obsession with the seemingly indifferent girl reworks Jacobus' own scandalous infatuation with Alice's mother, an exotic circus performer, whose story the narrator is ironically aware of. The narrator, however, seems engulfed by forces beyond his control as his all-consuming desire for Alice leads to the collapse of self-control and dignity. As he brutally forces kisses on her, the seemingly passive Alice suddenly metamorphoses into a mermaid-like figure:

> with a downward, undulating, serpentine motion, a quick sliding dive, she got away from me smoothly. It was all very swift; I saw her pick up the tail of her wrapper and run for the door at the end of the verandah not very gracefully. (70)

The references, combined with an apparent lack of decorum on land, reinforce the mermaid image, and the word "serpentine" transforms Alice into a sinister, even intentionally malicious temptress. Certainly her effect on the narrator is destructive as self-disgust overwhelms him: "It was like being the slave of some depraved habit" (59). She also severs his connection with the sea: "I wanted to stay for one more experience of that strange provoking sensation and of indefinite desire, the habit of which had made me – me of all people! – dread the prospect of going to sea" (73). The mermaid parallel, however, suggests that she also represents the sea, playing with, testing, and even victimizing one of its own. The thriving of Jacobus' potatoes, purchased out of guilt, seems to reinforce this alliance as the ship and sea nurture the narrator's shame. The mermaid-enchantress turns the narrator into another kind of liminal being, devoted to the sea yet unable to live upon it, handing in his resignation in despair, trapped in a tortuous mental state of perpetual dissatisfaction and regret.

Just as the "brute" is incapable of speech, however, there is no entry into Alice's feelings. She exists, apparently, to torment and cause a rift between the captain and "the ship I had learned to love" (88), but it is Jacobus who actually invites and encourages the narrator in a typical circulation of female energy among males. Alice might thus be seen as another victim of the male mythology of the temptress. The mermaid is another convenient scapegoat for a male crisis of confidence. These powerful images appear, therefore, when male characters fail to live up to their ideals of honour, courage, and strength. The reader suspects that the captain abandons his ship not only through self-disgust but also because he fears the consequences of his betrayal. In "A Smile of Fortune," the narrator's resentment at having been tricked and mocked is finally outweighed by an awareness of his culpability. After all, he seems destined to become another Marlow.

The notion of male blame is further developed in "Freya of the Seven Isles" where the beautiful young heroine is abandoned by her lover, Jasper. Freya is blond, "self-reliant" (179), and capable whereas Alice is dark and ethereal, but they share the same ability to capture and enslave. Freya's musical talents and island home make her another siren seemingly controlling the waters:

> Freya would sit down to the piano and play fierce Wagner music in the flicker of blinding flashes, with thunderbolts falling all round … and Jasper would remain stock still on the verandah, adoring the back view of her supple, swaying figure, the miraculous sheen of her fair head, the rapid hands on the keys, the white nape of her neck – while the brig, down at the point there, surged at her cables within a hundred yards of nasty, shiny, black rock-heads. (152)

The brig's dangerous position makes Freya's position ambiguous, suggesting both a dance with, and an attack on, the ship. The admiring narrator suggests the former, wondering whether she was born at sea and admiring her abilities as a sailor. Moreover, Jasper's love of Freya is intricately bound up in his love for the brig that is to be their home, a fusion of woman, ship, and sea: "His feelings for the brig and for the girl were as indissolubly united in his heart as you may fuse two precious metals together in one crucible. And the flame was pretty hot, I can assure you" (158). The narrator, glad not to feel this flame, recognizes the dangers inherent in over-romanticizing this attachment. The "flame" even suggests a challenge to the sea. Jasper and Freya seem too careless and complacent, disregarding or ignoring the precariousness of their position, opposed by her father, resented by Van Heemskirk, and surrounded by volatile, potentially jealous, waters.

Whereas the reader is unable to judge the extent of Alice's awareness and involvement in "A Smile of Fortune," Freya, by contrast, is unconscious of her influence and unprepared for the devastating consequences that follow her taunting of the jealous Van Heemskirk. Alice is constantly accompanied by a sinister older woman who arouses immediate paranoia in the narrator – "She was, I perceived, armed with a knitting-needle; and as she raised her hand her intention seemed to be to throw it at me like a dart" (48) – but Freya is isolated from an instructive female influence. Her violent piano playing, with its distinctly sexual overtones of rapture and fulfilment, represents an instinctual moment of madness: "She was excited, she tingled all over, she had tasted blood" (205). The power of the siren-song seems to overwhelm her as her father's voice is "nearly drowned by the piano" (206), and she comes to regret her actions: "she bowed her fair head, feeling a sudden discontent, a nervous lassitude, as though she had passed through some exhausting crisis" (207).

Van Heemskirk wrecks the brig in spite and revenge, using the sea as a weapon, leaving Jasper a broken man. Like the narrator of "A Smile of Fortune," he becomes estranged from the sea, unable to live up to Freya's or his own ideals. Paradoxically, however, Freya also seems to become isolated. Her fatal pneumonia even seems a punishment for an abuse of power, as she mournfully tells her father: "Draw the curtain, papa. Shut the sea out. It reproaches me with my folly" (238). Foolish or not, the narrator's sympathies lie with the tragic Freya, dangerously repressed and finally destroyed by the petty jealousies and inadequacies of the men surrounding her. The narrator's sadness seems to represent the final stage in a cycle as the relationship between man, woman, and sea gradually develops from defiance and counterattack to resentment, guilt, alienation, and regret. As Jasper watches his brig being towed away, his by now indistinguishable dependence on the vessel and on Freya emphasizes his ineffectiveness: the brig "his cherished possession, animated by something of his Freya's soul, [is] the only foothold of two lives on the wide earth, the security of his passion, the companion of adventure, the power to snatch the calm, adorable Freya to his breast, and carry her off to the end of the world" (218). In his arrogant, unthinking desire to keep both ship and girl, Jasper destroys both.

In Conrad's short stories, an over-investment in traditional male mythologies can leave the sailor, like the lover, irreparably heartbroken. Conrad seems to reverse the traditional model of male dominance over this sphere by suggesting that an unswerving loyalty to the sea/ship is both natural and fitting and even seems to advocate the Victorian work ethic as idleness and distraction become the seaman's true enemy. Indeed, he remained a stalwart defender of sail in the great debate about steam precisely because of its more feminine, ethereal, difficult qualities: "The sailing-ship, with her unthrobbing body, seemed to lead mysteriously a sort of unearthly existence, bordering upon the magic of the invisible forces, sustained by the inspiration of life-giving and death-dealing winds" (*Mirror of the Sea* 64). Femininity becomes a metaphor for all that disrupts a patriarchal attempt at control, while female characters emphasize the weaknesses of Conrad's heroes. Yet "petticoats" remain a necessary foil for male complacency. Their absence in "The Secret

Sharer" might even account for its morally dubious conclusion as the captain-narrator imperils his ship and crew to save Leggatt from the law. As Singleton says in *The Nigger of the "Narcissus,"* in words almost identical to those of the "elderly respectable seaman" (131) Conrad meets in *The Mirror of the Sea*: "Ships are all right. It is the men in them!" (24).

Works cited

Conrad, Joseph. *Collected Edition of the Works of Joseph Conrad.* 22 vols. London: J. M. Dent & Sons, 1946-1955.

Jean-Aubry, G., ed. *Joseph Conrad: Life and Letters.* 2 vols. London: Heinemann, 1927.

Jones, Susan. *Conrad and Women.* Oxford: Oxford University Press, 1999.

Knowles, Owen, and Gene M. Moore. *Oxford Reader's Companion to Conrad.* Oxford University Press, 2000.